# CELEBRATE EVERY SEASON
## ~ WITH ~
# six sisters' *stuff*

### 150+ Recipes, Traditions, and Fun Ideas for Each Month of the Year

SHADOW
MOUNTAIN

To our families

for always supporting us and for

being our taste testers, good and bad!

All photographs courtesy SixSistersStuff.com, except the following photographs: typography on the title page © Idea Trader/Shutterstock.com; books on page 37 © Pigprox/Shutterstock.com; place setting on page 37 © Daria Minaeva/Shutterstock.com; Indian food on page 38 © norikko/Shutterstock.com; video game controllers on page 38 © wavebreakmedia/Shutterstock.com; couple with face masks on page 38 © varuna/Shutterstock.com; St. Patrick's Day hat on page 54 © Mega Pixel/Shutterstock.com; popsicles on page 115 © marcin jucha/Shutterstock.com; miniature golf on page 115 © Andrey_Kuzmin/Shutterstock.com; barbecue on page 115 © TORWAISTUDIO/Shutterstock.com; flowers on page 116 © Alexander Raths/Shutterstock.com; cookies on page 116 © viennetta/Shutterstock.com; puppets on page 116 © Africa Studio/Shutterstock.com; water slide on page 116 © Rob Hainer/Shutterstock.com; family in tent on page 116 © oliveromg/Shutterstock.com; roller blades on page 116 © hurricanehank/Shutterstock.com; s'mores on page 135 © Arina P Habich/Shutterstock.com; foam floor tiles on page 136 © Masterchief_Productions/Shutterstock.com; cooler on page 136 © Dr Ajay Kumar Singh/Shutterstock.com; pill box on page 136 © Tyler Stuard/Shutterstock.com.

Visit us at ShadowMountain.com

**Library of Congress Cataloging-in-Publication Data**

Names: Six Sisters' Stuff, issuing body.
Title: Celebrate every season with Six Sisters' Stuff : 150+ recipes, traditions, and fun ideas for each month of the year / Six Sisters' Stuff.
Description: Salt Lake City, Utah : Shadow Mountain, [2017] | Includes index.
Identifiers: LCCN 2016059104 | ISBN 9781629723280 (paperbound)
Subjects: LCSH: Seasonal cooking. | LCGFT: Cookbooks.
Classification: LCC TX714 .C42865 2017 | DDC 641.5/64—dc23
LC record available at https://lccn.loc.gov/2016059104

Printed in China
RR Donnelley, Shenzhen, China

10   9   8   7   6   5   4   3   2   1

# CONTENTS

## March
*Recipes to Get Your Green On*

## April
*Recipes for Easter Dinner*

## November

*Recipes for a Thanksgiving Feast*

## December

*Festive Recipes for a Merry Christmas*

# JANUARY

## *Recipes to Ring in the New Year*

# Snowmen on a Stick

Yield: 6 snowmen on a stick | Prep time: 20 minutes | Cook time: n/a | Total time: 20 minutes

6   regular-sized marshmallows

6   (12-inch) skewers, plus one to use during assembly

1   cup milk chocolate chips

6   chocolate wafer cookies, such as Oreos, with crème filling removed

18  mini powdered donuts

½   cup fruit candies, such as Mike and Ike candies

¼   cup mini chocolate chips, for eyes and mouth

2   Fruit Roll-Ups, cut into strips ¾-inch wide

6   flower-shaped candy sprinkles (optional)

Place a marshmallow on the blunt end of each skewer and set aside while melting chocolate.

In a microwave-safe bowl, melt milk chocolate chips on high power in 30-second intervals until smooth, stirring often.

Dip each marshmallow in the melted chocolate and tap off any excess chocolate. Place the skewers, marshmallow side up, in a tall glass so the chocolate can set; set aside.

With a small paring knife, make a small hole in the center of each chocolate wafer. Dip each chocolate wafer cookie in the melted chocolate and tap off any excess chocolate; place on parchment paper to set up. (Alternatively, place in the refrigerator about 10 minutes for faster setting.)

Remove a skewer from the glass and turn it upside down so marshmallow is resting on a piece of parchment paper. Slide a dipped wafer cookie onto each skewer until it is flush against the marshmallow.

Carefully slide 3 donuts onto the skewer. Cut a fruit candy in half and slide it against the last donut to hold them all in place.

Lay the skewer on a piece of parchment paper and then use the sharp end of another skewer to poke tiny holes in the top donut for eyes and a mouth. Put mini chocolate chips, pointed ends in, in each hole.

Add ½ of an orange candy to the top donut for a nose. Stick red and green candy halves in the bottom two donuts for the buttons.

Carefully stretch one of the ¾-inch pieces of Fruit Roll-Ups until it is about 6 inches long. Wrap it around the snowman's neck and then trim the end of the scarf with scissors.

If desired, add a flower sprinkle to the snowman's hat using melted chocolate to hold it in place.

# Pineapple Cheeseball

Serves: 10 | Prep time: 15 minutes | Chill time: 3 hours | Total time: 3 hours, 10 minutes

2 (8-ounce) bricks cream cheese, softened

1 (8-ounce) can crushed pineapple, drained

¼ cup minced green bell pepper

2 tablespoons minced green onions

2 teaspoons seasoning salt

1 cup coarsely chopped pecans

Crackers, for serving

In a large mixing bowl, combine cream cheese, crushed pineapple, green pepper, green onions, seasoning, and salt.

Form into a ball, place on a plate, and cover with plastic wrap; refrigerate 3 hours or overnight, until firm and chilled.

Just before serving, place chopped pecans in a shallow bowl and roll cheese ball in pecans to coat.

Serve with crackers.

# Mock Champagne

Serves: 16 | Prep time: 5 minutes | Cook time: n/a | Total time: 5 minutes

- 1 (11.5-ounce) can white grape juice frozen concentrate, partially thawed
- 1½ cups water
- 1 (2-liter) bottle ginger ale

In a large punch bowl, mix together white grape juice concentrate, water, and ginger ale. Serve immediately and enjoy!

# Raspberry Frappé

Serves: 15 | Prep time: 15 minutes | Cook time: n/a | Total time: 15 minutes

- 1.5 quarts vanilla ice cream, slightly softened
- 1.5 quarts raspberry sherbet, slightly softened
- 1 (2-liter) bottle lemon-lime soda

Scoop the ice cream and sherbet into a large punch bowl.

Slowly pour in the soda and stir gently. Let mixture sit 5 minutes to melt just a bit.

Stir again to blend the ice creams together. There should be some ice cream chunks in the drink.

# Slow Cooker Chili Cheese Dip

Serves: 8 to 10 | Prep time: 5 minutes | Cook time: 3 to 4 hours | Total time: 4 hours, 5 minutes

1 (15-ounce) can chili

1 cup salsa

1 (8-ounce) brick cream cheese, room temperature

1 cup shredded cheddar cheese, plus additional for garnishing

1 clove garlic, minced

1 onion, diced

Green onions (optional)

Spray the ceramic insert of a 3- to 4-quart slow cooker with nonstick cooking spray. Place all ingredients except additional cheese and green onions in slow cooker and mix well. Cook on low 3 to 4 hours, or until completely heated through, stirring twice during cooking time.

Stir well before serving and top with additional shredded cheese and chopped green onions if desired. Serve with chips or your favorite crackers or vegetables.

# Shrimp Taco Bites

Serves: 12, 2 taco bites per person | Prep time: 20 minutes | Cook time: 8 minutes | Total time: 28 minutes

2  pounds (12 to 15 count) raw shrimp, peeled and deveined

1  teaspoon salt

1  teaspoon cumin

2  teaspoons chili powder

   Zest of 1 lime

2  Roma tomatoes, chopped

1  avocado, chopped

1  tablespoon chopped cilantro

2  teaspoons lime juice

5  green onions, chopped

2½  cups sour cream

24  scoop-style tortilla chips

Preheat oven to 350 degrees F. Spray a large baking sheet with nonstick cooking spray
Spread shrimp out over prepared baking sheet.

In a small bowl, combine salt, cumin, chili powder, and lime zest; sprinkle cumin and chili powder mixture over shrimp.

Bake 5 to 8 minutes or until shrimp has turned pink and curls into itself slightly.

While shrimp cooks, combine tomatoes, avocado, and cilantro in a medium bowl. Toss with lime juice and set aside.

In a separate bowl, mix together chopped green onions and sour cream.

To assemble, fill half of one scoop-style chip with salsa mixture and the other half with sour cream mixture; top with one shrimp each.

# Southwest Baked Egg Rolls

Serves: 6 | Prep time: 15 minutes | Cook time: 25 minutes | Total time: 40 minutes

1 tablespoon vegetable oil

2 tablespoons minced green onion

2 tablespoons minced red bell pepper

⅓ cup frozen corn

¼ cup canned black beans, drained and rinsed

2 tablespoons frozen chopped spinach, thawed and drained

2 tablespoons diced jalapeño peppers, seeded if desired

1 chicken breast, cooked and finely diced

½ teaspoon ground cumin

½ teaspoon chili powder

½ teaspoon salt

Pinch cayenne pepper

¾ cup shredded Monterey Jack cheese

Egg roll wrappers

Preheat oven to 400 degrees F. Coat a baking sheet with nonstick cooking spray.

Heat olive oil in a large skillet over medium-high heat and sauté green onion and bell pepper just until soft, about 3 to 5 minutes.

Stir in the corn, black beans, spinach, and jalapeño peppers, cooking to heat through.

Add the diced chicken, cumin, chili powder, salt, and cayenne pepper.

Stir until well blended.

Remove from heat and stir in the cheese.

Fill egg roll wrappers: add about ¼ cup filling to the center of the wrapper. Fold the corner nearest you over the filling, tuck in the sides, and finish rolling.

Place the rolls on prepared baking sheet and spray with nonstick cooking spray. Bake 20 minutes, flipping halfway through, until golden brown.

Serve with your favorite dipping sauces, such as chipotle sauce, salsa, ranch, and sour cream.

# Cowboy Caviar

Serves: 8 | Prep time: 10 minutes | Cook time: n/a | Total time: 10 minutes

5 to 6 Roma tomatoes, diced

1 (15-ounce) can black beans, drained and rinsed

1 (14-ounce) can corn, drained

½ medium onion, diced

1 avocado, diced

1 green bell pepper, diced

2 tablespoons diced jalapeños (more or less, according to taste)

½ teaspoon garlic powder

¾ cup Italian dressing

½ cup chopped fresh cilantro

Tortilla chips, for serving

In a large bowl, gently toss together tomatoes, black beans, corn, onion, avocado, green pepper, and jalapeños. Sprinkle garlic powder on top, then stir in dressing and cilantro. Serve with tortilla chips.

# Sweet Polynesian Meatballs

Yield: About 3 dozen meatballs | Prep time: 20 Minutes | Cook time: 60 minutes | Total time: 1 hour, 20 minutes

1 tablespoon olive oil

1 small onion, minced

1 teaspoon salt, divided

2 cloves garlic, minced

2 pinches crushed red pepper flakes, divided

1½ pounds ground beef

⅔ cup bread crumbs

⅔ cup milk

2 eggs, beaten

½ teaspoon dried parsley

½ teaspoon pepper

1 (12-ounce) bottle chili sauce

½ cup grape jelly

Preheat oven to 350 degrees F. Spray a 9x13-inch pan with cooking spray.

Heat oil in a large sauté pan over medium-high heat. Add onions, sprinkle with ½ teaspoon salt, and cook 5 to 7 minutes, until onions are soft and almost translucent. Add the garlic and 1 pinch crushed red pepper flakes and sauté another 1 to 2 minutes. Turn off heat, set aside, and allow to cool.

In a large bowl, combine ground beef, bread crumbs, milk, eggs, parsley, remaining ½ teaspoon salt, pepper, and 1 pinch crushed red pepper. Stir in cooled onion mixture.

Mix well and form into golf-ball-sized meatballs.

Place the meatballs in rows in prepared pan and set aside.

In a small saucepan, combine the chili sauce and grape jelly over medium heat and stir occasionally 5 to 6 minutes, or until it starts to bubble. Pour sauce over meatballs and bake 1 hour.

Serve over quinoa, brown rice, or white rice with a side of steamed vegetables.

# TRADITIONS

## New Year's Eve Family Countdown

Now that we have children, our New Year's Eve parties are geared toward the kid crowd rather than the adults in the house. When our children were really young, we would throw a New Year's Eve party that began early in the morning and counted down—or up, really—to noon. This outline is built around a 6 p.m. start time, but feel free to do an early morning to noon countdown instead if you'd like.

Before your guests arrive, write down each activity listed below on a small slip of paper. Fold each paper and place it in a balloon. Blow up the balloon, tie the end, and then label the balloon with the time that corresponds to the activity described on the paper. Use a Sharpie or other permanent marker to label each balloon. Then use your creativity to make a balloon arch, banner, or other design in the room. Choose someone to pop each balloon when the labeled time rolls around, and then have everyone participate in the activity listed inside.

Here is a sample list of activities for the night:

**6 p.m.**—Midnight pizza. Roll out your favorite homemade or store-bought dough into a large circle. Top pizza with sauce and cheese. Line the outside of the pizza with 12 pepperoni slices, placed where the numbers on a clock would be. Then use black olive slices to make the hands of the "clock" point to midnight. Let the kids help as much as possible!

**7 p.m.**—Game time. Let the kids pick some of their favorite board games to play together as a family.

**8 p.m.**—A cookies-and-milk toast. Pour yourself a fancy glass of milk and top with a chocolate chip cookie, then make a toast to the new year! If you want, let the kids help you make the cookies first and then finish off the hour with a milk-and-cookie toast.

**9 p.m.**—Annual video interview. Sit each kid down and interview them about the past year. Record the interviews with your smartphone or other recording device and then watch the previous year's video together. Here are some sample interview questions:

What is your name?

How old are you?

What grade are you in?

Who is your teacher?

What was the best thing about [current year]?

What is something you can't live without?

What is your favorite TV show?

What is your favorite food?

What is your favorite book?

What is your favorite animal?

What is your favorite subject at school?

What is your favorite toy?

What do you want to be when you grow up?

What is one thing you hope to do in [upcoming year]?

Where do you want to live when you grow up?

If you could go on a vacation anywhere, where would it be?

**10 p.m.**—Homemade party poppers. This is a fun craft the kids can make and then use at midnight!

You'll need colorful tissue paper, empty toilet-paper rolls, string or ribbon, candy, and confetti. To make the poppers, follow these steps:

1. Cut the tissue paper into a 10-inch square.

2. Place the toilet-paper roll in the center of one edge of the tissue paper and then wrap the paper tightly around the roll.

3. Gather the tissue paper on one end of the roll and twist it tightly; secure the end with a string or ribbon.

4. From the other end, fill the toilet-paper roll with candy and confetti and then secure that end in the same fashion as step 3.

5. To open, pull hard on both ends at the same time and watch the contents fly!

**11 p.m.**—Sparkler time. Bundle up—unless you're lucky to live somewhere warm—and take the kids outside to light sparklers.

**11:45 p.m.**—Showtime: Have everyone grab their noise makers, poppers, pots and pans, whistles, and whatever else they want to use to joyfully ring in the New Year! Get glasses of sparkling cider or our Mock Champagne ready so you can have another toast after the countdown.

# FEBRUARY

## Recipes to Share with Your Sweetheart

# Red Velvet Crepes

Serves: 20 | Prep time: 15 minutes | Cook time: 15 minutes | Total time: 30 minutes

1½  cups all-purpose flour

1  teaspoon baking powder

½  teaspoon baking soda

5  tablespoons granulated sugar

2  cups buttermilk

1½  cups milk

1  large egg

1  teaspoon vanilla extract

2  tablespoons unsweetened cocoa powder

1  tablespoon red food coloring

3  tablespoons butter, melted

Dash salt

Whipped cream cheese, for filling

Whipped cream, for filling

Nutella or chocolate sauce, for filling

Sliced strawberries, for filling

Powdered sugar, for garnishing

In a large bowl, whisk together the flour, baking powder, baking soda, and sugar until fully combined; set aside.

In a separate bowl, mix the buttermilk, milk, egg, vanilla extract, cocoa powder, food coloring, butter, and salt until well combined.

Pour liquid mixture into the bowl with the dry ingredients.

Whisk together the wet and dry ingredients until well combined and only a few small lumps remain.

The mixture should be smooth and quite a bit thinner than pancake batter. Add a tablespoon or 2 of milk if the batter seems too thick.

Heat a medium skillet over medium heat, spray with nonstick cooking spray, and then pour ¼ cup of the crepe batter into the hot pan.

Lift and tilt the pan in a circular motion so the batter spreads evenly across the bottom of the pan.

Cook each crepe 30 seconds to 1 minute on each side and remove to paper-towel-lined plate while preparing the remaining batter.

Serve with cream cheese, whipped cream, Nutella, chocolate sauce, strawberries, or powdered sugar.

# Chocolate Raspberry Crepes

Serves: 6 | Prep time: 15 minutes | Cook time: 5 minutes | Total time: 20 minutes

1 cup all-purpose flour

2 eggs (or 4 egg whites)

½ cup water

½ cup milk

¼ teaspoon salt

2 tablespoons butter, melted

1 (3-ounce) package instant chocolate pudding mix, prepared with 2 cups milk as directed on package

½ to 1 cup raspberries, according to taste

Powdered sugar, for garnishing

Whipped cream, for garnishing

In a large mixing bowl, whisk together flour, eggs, water, and milk. Add salt and butter. Continue mixing until all lumps have disappeared

Heat a large skillet over medium heat and then spray with nonstick cooking spray.

Drop ¼ cup batter onto the heated pan. Immediately after batter is poured on, pick up the pan and tilt it in a circular motion so the batter covers the entire surface of the pan. Crepes will be very thin.

Cook about 2 minutes on the first side, flip, and cook another minute on the second side. Place crepe on paper-towel-lined plate and repeat until all batter is used.

Once pudding is setting up, stir in the raspberries and mix well. The raspberries may fall apart while stirring, but that is fine as it adds more raspberry flavor to each bite.

Spoon filling on each crepe, roll it up, and sprinkle the top with powdered sugar and whipped cream.

# Strawberry-Lemonade Cake Bites

Yield: 50 cake bites | Prep time: 45 minutes | Cook time: 30 minutes | Total time: 1 hour 15 minutes

1   (15.25-ounce) strawberry cake mix, prepared according to package directions and cooled completely

1   (16-ounce) tub lemon frosting

1   pound white chocolate candy melts or almond bark

1   (6-ounce) bag pink candy melts

Cover baking sheets with parchment or waxed paper and set aside.

Using your hands, crumble the baked and cooled cake into a large bowl. Stir in the container of frosting, ½ cup at a time, until mixture is a nice consistency that will hold together when rolled into a ball.

Roll the mashed cake into ¾-inch balls, then smash each ball down to form a disk shape. Place bites on prepared baking sheets and chill 30 minutes to firm up.

Melt white chocolate candy coating or almond bark according to directions on back of package. Use a skewer to pierce, lift, and then dip each ball in the melted white chocolate. Rotate each bite a couple of times to make sure it is evenly covered with chocolate.

Return each bite to the prepared pans and let them set up 15 to 20 minutes. Melt pink candy melts according to package directions and then spoon melted candy into a zipper-top sandwich bag. Clip off a very tiny corner on the bag and then pipe the melted pink candy over each bite.

# Valentine Sugar Cookies

Yield: 48 to 60 cookies | Prep time: 2 hours 15 minutes | Cook time: 7 minutes | Total time: 2 hours 22 minutes

6 cups all-purpose flour

1 teaspoon baking soda

1 teaspoon baking powder

½ teaspoon salt

1 cup unsalted butter, at room
temperature

2 cups granulated sugar

3 large eggs

2 teaspoons vanilla extract

1½ cups sour cream

1 recipe Buttercream Frosting
Sprinkles (optional)

In a large bowl whisk together flour, baking soda, baking powder, and salt; set aside.

With an electric mixer, cream the butter and sugar together at medium speed until light and fluffy, about 3 minutes. Add the eggs, one at a time, beating well after each addition. Add the vanilla extract and sour cream and mix at a low speed until combined.

Add the dry ingredients and beat at low speed until just combined. Dough will be a little sticky, but that is okay. Divide dough into two sections. Flatten into rectangles about 1½ inches thick, then wrap each with plastic wrap. Chill in the refrigerator overnight or for at least 2 hours.

When ready to shape and bake cookies, preheat oven to 425 degrees F.

Lightly flour the countertop and the top of the dough. With a rolling pin, roll the dough out to a ¼-inch thickness. Using cookie cutters, cut out the cookies and place on ungreased baking sheets. Bake 7 minutes, until cookies are slightly golden around the edges. Immediately transfer cookies to a wire rack to cool. Let the cookies cool completely before frosting with Buttercream Frosting and top with sprinkles if desired.

When frosting is set, store leftover cookies in an airtight container.

## Buttercream Frosting

1   cup unsalted butter, room temperature

1   teaspoon vanilla extract

4   cups powdered sugar

Pinch salt

6   tablespoons heavy cream

Food coloring (optional)

In a large bowl with an electric mixer, cream together the butter and vanilla extract. Slowly beat in powdered sugar and the pinch of salt. Once mixture is very smooth and creamy, add in heavy cream, 1 tablespoon at a time. When cream has all been incorporated, beat at medium-high speed for 1 to 2 minutes, until light and fluffy. Add a few drops food coloring, if desired, and beat until combined.

# Red Velvet Bundt Cake with Cream Cheese Frosting

Serves: 10 | Prep time: 15 minutes | Cook time: 45 minutes | Total time: 1 hour

- 1 (15.25-ounce) box red velvet cake mix
- 2 (3-ounce) boxes instant chocolate pudding mix
- ½ cup vegetable oil
- 1¼ cups water
- 4 eggs
- 1 recipe Cream Cheese Frosting

Preheat oven to 350 degrees F. Spray a 10-inch bundt pan with nonstick cooking spray.

In a large mixing bowl, combine cake mix, pudding mixes, oil, water, and eggs until well incorporated.

Pour batter into prepared bundt pan and bake 40 to 45 minutes, or until a toothpick inserted in center comes out clean. Let cake cool for 10 minutes, then invert onto a serving plate to finish cooling.

Spread or pipe Cream Cheese Frosting onto cooled cake.

## Cream Cheese Frosting

- ¼ cup butter, at room temperature
- 1 (8-ounce) brick cream cheese, at room temperature
- 1 teaspoon vanilla extract
- 3 cups powdered sugar

In a large bowl, with an electric mixer on high speed, cream together butter, cream cheese, and vanilla until smooth. Add powdered sugar a little at a time until frosting reaches desired consistency.

# Mini Red Velvet Cheesecakes

Yield: 16 mini cheesecakes | Prep Time: 2 hours | Cook Time: 30 minutes | Total time: 2 hours, 30 minutes

20  Oreo cookies, white filling removed

4  tablespoons butter, melted

2½  (8-ounce) bricks cream cheese, room temperature

⅔  cup granulated sugar

¼  cup unsweetened cocoa powder

2  teaspoons vanilla extract

2  tablespoons red food coloring

2  eggs

1  cup heavy cream

4  tablespoons powdered sugar

1  (1.55-ounce) Hershey's Milk Chocolate Bar, curled (see note)

Preheat oven to 350 degrees F. Place foil cupcake liners into 16 regular-sized muffin cups.

Crush the Oreo cookies and add to a small bowl. Combine crumbs and melted butter until well incorporated. Divide the mixture evenly between the 16 foil-lined muffin cups. Press the crumbs firmly into each foil liner with your fingers or the back of a spoon. Bake 5 minutes, then remove from oven to cool on a wire rack.

In a large bowl, beat the cream cheese with an electric mixer on high speed until smooth. Gradually add the granulated sugar and cocoa powder and beat until fluffy. Beat in vanilla and food coloring. Then add eggs, one at a time, and beat until well blended.

Spoon the batter equally between the muffin cups, filling each cup about ¾ full. You may have a little batter left over, but you do not want to overfill the cups.

Bake 23 to 25 minutes, then turn off the oven, but leave cheesecakes in the oven an additional 15 minutes with door closed. Carefully remove from the oven and leave at room temperature on the counter another 30 minutes. This will help the cheesecakes from falling in the middle; although the center will still sink a little.

Once cooled, transfer cheesecakes to the refrigerator and chill for an hour. When completely cooled, remove the cupcake liner from each individual cheesecake.

In a small bowl, with an electric mixer, beat cream and powdered sugar on high speed until stiff. Spoon or pipe the whipped cream on top of each cheesecake and then garnish with chocolate curls. Store in the refrigerator in an airtight container.

*Note:* To make chocolate curls, hold candy bar on end. Using a vegetable peeler, hold it against the edge of the bar and pull toward you in long, thin strokes. For smaller curls, use the short edge of the candy bar.

# Heart-Shaped Valentine's Cupcakes

Yield: About 24 cupcakes | Prep time: 10 minutes | Cook time: 15 minutes | Total time: 25 minutes

1 recipe favorite cake batter or batter prepared from a mix, according to package directions

Marbles (see note)

Frosting

Sprinkles

Preheat oven as directed in chosen cake recipe or according to package directions.

Line a muffin pan with paper liners. Scoop batter into liners about ⅔ full. Do not overfill. After filling the liners, place a marble between the liner and the pan at the top center of the cupcake. The marble will make the cupcake take on the shape of a heart. Bake according to package or recipe directions.

Cool completely and decorate with frosting and sprinkles.

*Note:* Marbles can be purchased at the dollar store. If you don't have marbles, you could roll up small balls of aluminum foil instead.

# Raspberry White Chocolate Chip Cookies

Yield: 12 large cookies | Prep time: 20 minutes | Cook time: 22 minutes | Total time: 42 minutes

½ cup butter, at room temperature
½ cup brown sugar
⅓ cup granulated sugar
1 egg
1 egg yolk
1 teaspoon vanilla extract
½ teaspoon almond extract

2 cups all-purpose flour
2 teaspoons cornstarch
1 teaspoon baking soda
¼ teaspoon salt
¾ cup white chocolate chips
¾ cup chocolate chips
3 tablespoons seedless raspberry jam

Preheat oven to 350 degrees F. Line baking sheets with parchment paper.

In a large bowl with an electric mixer, cream together butter and sugars until light and fluffy. Add egg, egg yolk, vanilla, and almond extract and mix until combined.

Add in flour, cornstarch, baking soda, and salt and beat until combined.

Fold in the chocolate chips and white chips.

Separate the dough in half. Put 1 half on a plate and spread it out with your hands into a 1-inch thick disk. Dot the dough with half of the jam and then use a knife to cut—but not stir—the jam into the dough.

Roll 2 to 3 tablespoons dough into a ball and repeat to make 6 dough balls.

Place balls on prepared baking sheet, gently press down on the top of each cookie, and then chill in the refrigerator 15 minutes.

Repeat with second half of dough while first batch chills.

Remove first batch from refrigerator and bake 11 to 12 minutes. Chill second batch of dough while first is baking.

Let baked cookies cool on the baking sheet 5 minutes, and then remove to wire rack to cool completely.

# White Chocolate Pretzel Hearts

Serves: About 8 | Prep time: 25 minutes | Cook time: n/a | Total time: 25 minutes

48  mini pretzel twists

1  (8-ounce) package almond bark

Jumbo heart sprinkles or conversation hearts

Lay pretzels in a single layer on a piece of parchment paper.

Melt almond bark according to package directions and then transfer to a zipper-top bag. Cut a small hole in the corner of the bag and pipe the melted bark into the three open spaces on each pretzel; the pretzels will then look like hearts. Immediately place a jumbo heart candy or conversation heart into the center of each pretzel and press down lightly to set. Continue until all pretzels are filled. Let almond bark set about 40 to 45 minutes and then serve.

# Chocolate-Peanut Butter Hearts

Serves: 12 to 18 | Prep time: 1 hour, 15 minutes | Cook time: 3 minutes | Total time: 1 hour, 18 minutes

2 cups creamy peanut butter

3 cups powdered sugar

1 teaspoon vanilla extract

1 tablespoon milk

2 cups milk chocolate chips

Heart-shaped cookie cutter

Line a baking sheet with parchment or waxed paper.

In a large bowl with an electric mixer, combine peanut butter, powdered sugar, vanilla, and milk until well incorporated.

On a lightly floured surface, roll out the peanut butter mixture about ¼-inch thick. Use the cookie cutter—or freehand it with a knife—to cut out hearts in the dough. Place the peanut butter hearts on prepared baking sheet and freeze 1 hour.

Remove the peanut butter hearts from the freezer. In a medium, microwave-safe bowl, melt chocolate chips on high power in 30-second intervals, stirring after each, until smooth.

Use a fork to pierce the peanut butter hearts and dip them in the melted chocolate. Return hearts to prepared baking sheet and let chocolate harden before serving!

# TRADITIONS

## *Stay-at-Home Date Ideas*

With babies and young kids in the house, going out on the town for date nights can sometimes get tricky. These are fourteen dates you can have at home after the little ones are in bed:

**Homemade pizza night.** This is just what it sounds like. Roll out some dough, add your favorite toppings, bake, and enjoy.

**Book club for two.** A week or two in advance of date night, choose a book to read. On the date night, discuss the book's themes and plot.

**Romantic candlelight dinner.** After the kids go to bed, set out your finest tablecloth and china, light a few candles, and eat takeout in the candlelight.

**Theme night.** Select a theme for your date night and center everything on it. For example, if you chose an Italian theme you could eat spaghetti, watch a movie like *The Italian Job*, and then have gelato for dessert. For an Indian them, watch a Bollywood movie while eating a bowl of spicy coconut curry. For chocolate theme, watch the movie *Chocolat* and enjoy a variety of chocolate fondues.

**Play the Newlywed Game.** See how well you really know one another by writing down a list of questions together. Then take turns answering how you think your spouse would respond to each question.

**Living room campout.** Turn the living room into a campsite. Turn off the lights, use flashlights, cuddle up in sleeping bags, etc. Make tin foil dinners in the oven for dinner and s'mores over the stovetop or grill for dessert.

**Get a taste of another culture.** Plan a delicious meal with authentic recipes from another culture.

**Karaoke night.** Find songs with lyrics online and sing your hearts out! Find some love songs you can sing together as duets.

**Chocolate-tasting night.** Purchase a variety of different kinds of chocolate at the store and rate each one. Compare your ratings.

**Trilogy movie marathon.** Select a popular movie trilogy and have a movie marathon. Split this date into three nights if needed.

**Make a bucket list.** Write out a list of fifty things you want to do in your lifetime and share your list with each other. Decide together which ones you will tackle first!

**Video game night.** Video games aren't just for kids! Have a little friendly competition and play video games together.

**Play "Twenty Questions."** Create a list of twenty out-of-the-ordinary questions to ask your spouse to learn more about him or her.

**Stay-at-home spa night.** Make your home into a spa by giving each other massages and/or pedicures and indulging in homemade facials.

# MARCH

## *Recipes to Get Your Green On*

# St. Patrick's Day Cupcakes

Yield: 24 cupcakes | Prep time: 30 minutes | Cook time: 20 minutes | Total time: 50 minutes

24 baked, but not frosted, vanilla cupcakes

1 cup butter, softened

4½ cups powdered sugar

1 teaspoon vanilla extract

⅓ cup heavy cream

¼ teaspoon salt

Green food coloring

12 AirHeads Rainbow Berry Xtremes Sweet and Sour Candies

Mini-marshmallows

24 ROLO caramels

Gold sprinkles

Prepare the frosting: In a large bowl with an electric mixer on medium-high speed, beat butter until creamy, about 2 minutes. Add powdered sugar, vanilla, heavy cream, and salt and beat together until light and fluffy, about 3 minutes. Add green food coloring until desired color is reached.

Spread or pipe frosting on top of each cupcake.

Cut each AirHeads Rainbow Berry Xtreme candy in half and place on top of each cupcake to create an arch—or rainbow! Place two mini-marshmallows on each end of the rainbow for clouds. To make the pot of gold, pipe a small amount of frosting onto the wide end of each ROLO, then press into gold sprinkles until all the frosting is covered. Place on the cupcake, gold side up.

# Evergreen Party Punch

Serves: 20 to 30 | Prep time: 5 minutes | Cook time: n/a | Total time: 5 minutes

2 (0.13-ounce) packets lemon-lime Kool-Aid Unsweetened Drink Mix

2 cups granulated sugar

8 cups water

1 (2-liter) bottle lemon-lime soda

½ gallon lime, pineapple, or lemon sherbet, slightly softened

1 (46-ounce) container pineapple juice

Ice

Combine all ingredients except for the ice in a large punch bowl. Stir in ice to keep drink cold and serve immediately.

# Shamrock Shake

Serves: 2 | Prep time: 5 minutes | Cook time: n/a | Total time: 5 minutes

3 to 4   cups vanilla ice cream
    1   cup whole milk
    ½   teaspoon peppermint extract

    ¼   teaspoon green food coloring
        Whipped cream, for topping
        Green sprinkles, for topping

Place ice cream, milk, peppermint extract, and green food coloring in a blender. Cover and blend until smooth. Pour into glasses and top with whipped cream and sprinkles. Serve immediately.

# St. Patrick's Day Puppy Chow

Serves: 10 | Prep time: 10 minutes | Cook time: 2 minutes | Total time: 12 minutes

6 to 8   cups Corn Chex Cereal

2   cups green candy melts

3   cups powdered sugar, divided

Place Corn Chex Cereal in a large mixing bowl and set aside.

In a separate, microwave-safe bowl, melt candy on high power in 30-second intervals, stirring after each one, until smooth.

Pour the melted candy over the cereal and gently fold until the cereal is coated.

Scoop 1½ cups powdered sugar into each of 2 large, zipper-top plastic bags. Divide the candy-coated cereal between the 2 bags, seal, and shake until cereal is evenly coated with powdered sugar.

# Green Mac 'n' Cheese

Serves: 6 to 8 | Prep time: 20 minutes | Cook time: 20 minutes | Total time: 40 minutes

| | | | |
|---|---|---|---|
| 1 | pound elbow macaroni | ½ | cup water |
| 3 | cups milk | 4 | cups shredded white cheddar cheese |
| 1 | cup spinach | 2 | cups chopped broccoli florets |
| 3 | tablespoons butter | 1 | cup peas |
| 3 | tablespoons all-purpose flour | | |

Preheat oven to 350 degrees F.  Spray a 9x13-inch baking pan with nonstick cooking spray.

Cook pasta according to package directions until al dente. Drain and set aside.

While pasta is cooking, place milk and spinach in a blender and process until smooth; set aside.

In a large saucepan over medium heat, melt the butter until foamy and then whisk in flour, stirring 2 to 3 minutes, until mixture has a rich, nutty smell. Slowly whisk in the spinach and milk mixture and bring to a boil.

Reduce heat to low and cook 3 to 4 minutes, until sauce begins to thicken, whisking occasionally.

Add ½ cup water and the shredded cheese and whisk until melted. Stir in the pasta, broccoli, and peas.

Transfer sauce and noodles to prepared baking dish and bake 20 minutes, or until cheese is bubbling.

# Homemade Peppermint Patties

Yield: 28 patties | Prep time: 2 hours, 15 minutes | Cook time: n/a | Total time: 2 hours 15 minutes

¾ cup sweetened condensed milk

1½ teaspoons peppermint extract

4 cups powdered sugar

3 cups semisweet chocolate chips

2 teaspoons shortening

Line a baking sheet with parchment or waxed paper.

In a large mixing bowl, combine sweetened condensed milk and peppermint extract. With an electric mixer, beat in the powdered sugar, a little at a time, until a stiff dough starts to form and the dough is no longer sticky.

Form dough into 1-inch balls, then place on prepared baking sheet. Flatten each ball with fingers to form patties. Let patties dry at room temperature for 2 hours, flipping over after an hour to set evenly on both sides.

After 2 hours, place the pan in the freezer for 30 minutes. Meanwhile, melt chocolate and shortening in a saucepan over low heat, stirring often, until smooth. Remove chocolate from heat and let cool for a few minutes. Remove patties from freezer and dip them into the chocolate one at a time by resting them on the tines of a fork, covering both sides, and letting excess chocolate drip off. Place dipped patties back on the parchment or waxed paper and let cool until chocolate is set.

# 5-Minute Pistachio Salad

Serves: 6 | Prep time: 5 minutes | Cook time: n/a | Total time: 5 minutes

1 (20-ounce) can pineapple chunks or tidbits

1 (3-ounce) package instant pistachio pudding

1 (8-ounce) carton nondairy whipped topping, thawed

2 cups mini-marshmallows

2 bananas, sliced

Drain juice from canned pineapple into a large bowl. Pour pudding mix into the juice and mix well. Fold the whipped topping into the pudding. Add pineapple chunks and marshmallows and stir together gently. Top with sliced bananas.

# Rainbow Fruit Kebabs with Fluffy Marshmallow Dip

Serves: Varies, depending on how much fruit is used | Prep time: 15 minutes | Cook time: n/a | Total time: 15 minutes

Strawberries, halved

Cantaloupe, cut into bite-sized pieces

Pineapple, cut into bite-sized pieces

Green grapes

Blueberries

Red grapes

Bamboo skewers

1 (8-ounce) container whipped cream cheese

1 (7-ounce) container marshmallow crème

Thread fruit, 1 piece at a time, onto each skewer in this order: 1 half strawberry, 1 cube cantaloupe, 1 cube pineapple, 1 green grape, 2 blueberries, and 1 red grape; set skewers aside while making dip.

In a mixing bowl, beat together whipped cream cheese and marshmallow crème until smooth. Refrigerate until serving.

*Note:* Add green food coloring to the dip for an extra festive dish.

# Rainbow Jell-O Cups

Serves: 8 | Prep time: 5 hours | Cook time: n/a | Total time: 5 hours

5 (3-ounce) packages Jell-O, 1 each in red, orange, yellow, green, and blue

2½ cups sour cream

Water

Sweetened whipped cream

Sprinkles

Place 8 clear plastic cups on a baking sheet.

In a medium bowl, stir the package of red Jell-O into 1 cup boiling water until dissolved.

Pour half of the mixture into another bowl and set aside.

Whisk in ½ cup sour cream to the first bowl of Jell-O and then pour equal amounts into the 8 clear plastic cups. Place tray in refrigerator to chill 30 minutes.

In the meantime, whisk 3 tablespoons cold water into the other half of the Jell-O mixture and set aside again.

After the creamy layer of Jell-O has set up, remove from fridge, and pour the reserved half of the Jell-O equally over the tops of each Jell-O cup.

Return to refrigerator another 30 minutes.

Repeat with each color of Jell-O to make ten layers.

When final layer has set, top with a dollop of whipped cream and a pinch of sprinkles.

# TRADITIONS

## *Leprechaun Treasure Hunt*

We definitely gained our love for the holidays from our sweet mom. She was always doing fun and creative things to celebrate, and she passed her love for all holidays down to us. Let your kids in on some of that magic with this leprechaun hunt.

How to play: Write each clue listed below on a small strip of paper. If desired, add your own clues. Hide the clues around the house. At each clue's hiding place, leave a small pile of gold candy as evidence that a leprechaun has passed through with treasure.

Help your kids follow all of the clues and find the gold treasure at the end.

Begin the search with this introduction, followed by Clue #1: "I'm a tiny leprechaun who loves the color green. I came in a flash so I wouldn't be seen! I brought you some treasure, and as you've been told, if you follow my clues you might find some gold!"

### Clues

1. "It's cold in here, but the food doesn't mind! Your first clue's behind the milk: not too hard to find."

2. "The next hiding place is where people knock, but this sneaky leprechaun did not!"

3. "This leprechaun loves the color green and left your next clue in the place you get clean!"

4. "This leprechaun was in such a rush! He dropped some treasure and forgot to flush." (Put green food coloring in the toilet and gold candy around the toilet.)

5. "After all his hiding, he needed a rest, and this leprechaun like your mom's bed the best!"

6. "You found my gold and followed every clue. Always remember the best treasure is YOU!"

# APRIL

## *Recipes for Easter Dinner*

# No-Bake Chocolate Bird's Egg Nest Cookies

Yield: About 12 Bird's Nests | Prep time: 10 minutes | Cook time: n/a | Total time: 10 minutes

1 (11- to 12-ounce) bag milk chocolate chips

1 (11- to 12-ounce) bag butterscotch chips (see note)

1 (10- to 12-ounce) bag chow mein noodles

M&M's, jellybeans, Cadbury eggs, or any other kind of "egg-shaped" candy

In a large, microwave-safe bowl, melt the chocolate chips and butterscotch chips at 50 percent power in 60-second intervals, stirring between each interval. Repeat until chips are smoothly melted.

Stir in chow mein noodles until all noodles are coated.

Lay out parchment or waxed paper and drop large tablespoonsful of chocolate-coated noodles on to the paper. Shape each mound into a "bird's nest." Wash your hands well and then place a couple of egg-shaped candies on top of the chocolate nest. Let nests harden before serving.

*Note:* If you don't like butterscotch chips, switch them out for white chocolate chips, peanut butter chips, or a second bag of chocolate chips.

# Bacon Parmesan Green Beans

Serves: 6 | Prep time: 10 minutes | Cook time: 10 minutes | Total time: 20 minutes

¾ cup water

1 pound fresh green beans

1 tablespoon olive oil

⅓ cup finely chopped red onion

1 tablespoon lemon juice

1 teaspoon minced garlic

½ teaspoon onion salt

½ teaspoon garlic salt

Pepper to taste

⅓ cup grated Parmesan cheese

5 to 6 strips bacon, cooked and crumbled

Bring the ¾ cup water to a boil in a large skillet over medium-high heat. Add green beans and continue to boil 3 minutes. Cover skillet with a lid, reduce heat to low, and let beans steam 5 minutes.

Drain water off the beans and add olive oil, red onion, lemon juice, and minced garlic.

Increase the heat to medium and sauté the beans, garlic, and onions until they begin to turn translucent.

Add the onion salt, garlic salt, pepper, Parmesan cheese, and bacon until everything is heated through and well incorporated.

# Potato Rolls

Yield: 16 rolls | Prep time: 2 hours | Cook time: 12 minutes | Total time: 2 hours, 12 minutes

1 large russet potato, peeled and chopped

⅓ cup unsalted butter, softened

2 tablespoons granulated sugar

1 tablespoon honey

1 teaspoon salt

1 egg

1⅛ teaspoons instant yeast

½ cup milk, warmed

1½ cups all-purpose flour

1½ cups bread flour

In a small pan of water over medium-high heat, boil chopped potato until tender. Drain off cooking water, reserving ¼ cup for later use. Finely mash the potato and measure out ½ cup. Let cool to room temperature.

In the bowl of a stand mixer fitted with the paddle attachment, mix together the ½ cup mashed potato, butter, sugar, honey, salt, and egg on medium speed 2 minutes.

Combine yeast, warm milk, and reserved potato water in a small bowl and then pour into mixer bowl. Mix on low speed until incorporated.

Gradually add flours, about a ½ cup at a time, until a soft dough forms. Switch to the dough hook attachment and knead on low speed for 5 minutes, adding more flour if necessary to achieve a soft dough that is slightly tacky but not sticky.

Transfer the dough to a lightly oiled bowl, turning once to coat. Cover with plastic wrap and let rise in a warm place until doubled in bulk, about 60 to 90 minutes.

Line a baking sheet with parchment paper. Turn the dough out onto a lightly floured surface and punch it down. Separate into 16 equal pieces and shape into rolls.

Place rolls on prepared baking sheet, about 1½ inches apart. Sprinkle the rolls with a dusting of flour. Cover with a clean kitchen towel and let the dough rise again until the rolls have grown into each other, about 30 to 45 minutes.

Preheat oven to 400 degrees F.

Bake rolls 12 minutes, or until golden brown. Serve warm.

# Citrus Glazed Ham

Serves: 20 | Prep time: 10 minutes | Cook time: 1 hour, 45 minutes | Total time: 1 hour, 55 minutes

1 (10-pound) bone-in, precooked spiral-cut ham

1 cup orange marmalade

1 teaspoon ground mustard

½ teaspoon garlic powder

¼ teaspoon ground black pepper

¼ teaspoon ground cloves

Preheat oven to 325 degrees F.

Place ham in a large roasting pan.

In a small bowl, mix together marmalade and spices until completely blended. Brush half of the marmalade mixture over ham, gently separating the slices so mixture can reach middle of ham. Cover loosely with foil.

Bake 1 hour, basting every 15 to 20 minutes with leftover marmalade. After 1 hour, remove foil and brush with remaining marmalade mixture. Bake 45 minutes longer (no basting required for the last 45 minutes). Serve ham with pan drippings.

# Smashed Cheesy Potatoes

Serves: 10 | Prep time: 10 minutes | Cook time: 30 minutes | Total time: 40 minutes

2   pounds baby Yukon gold potatoes

3   tablespoons butter

¼   teaspoon black pepper

3   cloves garlic, minced

1   teaspoon Old Bay Seasoning

3   tablespoons olive oil

   Salt and pepper, to taste

2   tablespoons chopped chives

1   cup shredded Colby Jack cheese

Preheat oven to 450 degrees F.

Rinse and gently scrub potatoes. Cook the potatoes in boiling water until fork tender, about 15 to 20 minutes.

While the potatoes are boiling, in a small, microwave-safe mixing bowl combine the butter, black pepper, garlic, and Old Bay Seasoning. Heat on high power about 60 seconds, until butter is melted. Mix well.

Drain the potatoes and gently pat dry.

Mix the olive oil and salt and pepper in a medium sized bowl. Roll each potato in the olive oil mixture until completely coated.

Place the potatoes on a rimmed baking sheet and gently flatten each with the bottom of a drinking glass.

With a pastry brush, coat each smashed potato with the butter mixture.

Bake 5 minutes. Remove from oven, sprinkle with half of the chives and all of the cheese, followed by the last half of the chives. Return to oven and bake an additional 5 to 6 minutes, until cheese is melted and bubbly.

# White Chocolate Carrot Cheesecake Bars

Serves: 18 | Prep time: 25 minutes | Cook time: 30 minutes | Total time: 55 minutes

## Crust

- 3 cups crushed graham cracker crumbs
- ¼ cup butter, melted
- ½ cup sweetened, flaked coconut
- ¼ cup crushed walnuts

## Cheesecake Filling

- 2 (8-ounce) bricks cream cheese, at room temperature
- ⅔ cup granulated sugar
- 2 large eggs
- 2 teaspoons lemon juice
- 2 teaspoons vanilla extract
- ½ cup white chocolate chips
- 4 tablespoons caramel sauce

## Topping

- 1¼ cups all-purpose flour
- ¾ cup oats
- ¼ cup brown sugar
- ¼ cup granulated sugar
- ¼ teaspoon baking soda
- ¼ teaspoon ground cinnamon
- ¼ teaspoon nutmeg
- ¾ cup grated carrots
- ¼ cup flaked coconut
- ¼ cup raisins
- ¼ cup chopped walnuts
- ½ cup butter, at room temperature
- ½ teaspoon vanilla extract
- ½ cup butter, at room temperature
- ½ cup white chocolate chips

Preheat oven to 350 degrees F. Line a 9x13-inch pan with foil and set aside.

*For crust:* Crush graham cracker crumbs until they are as fine as sand. Pour crumbs in a medium bowl and stir in melted butter until crumbs are thoroughly coated. Stir in coconut and chopped walnuts to combine well and then press into the bottom of prepared pan. Make sure the crumbs completely cover the bottom of the pan; set aside while preparing cheesecake filling.

*For filling:* In a large bowl, with an electric mixer, beat together the cream cheese and sugar until smooth and creamy. Add eggs, one at a time, and mix until fully incorporated.

Mix in lemon juice and vanilla and blend until smooth. Fold in white chocolate chips with a rubber spatula or spoon.

Pour the cheesecake filling over the uncooked graham cracker crust and then drizzle with the caramel sauce. Use a butter knife to swirl the caramel sauce around the cheesecake until a marble effect is achieved. Set aside while preparing topping.

*For topping:* In a large bowl, whisk together flour, oats, brown sugar, sugar, baking soda, cinnamon, and nutmeg. Stir in carrots, coconut, raisins, walnuts, and vanilla extract and then cut in butter until mixture resembles coarse crumbs.

Lightly toss the crumbly carrot mixture over the cheesecake filling.

Bake about 45 minutes, until the carrot cake mixture is golden brown and the cheesecake jiggles just slightly in the middle but is otherwise set.

Remove from oven and top with the white chocolate chips. Cool slightly on a wire rack and then chill in the refrigerator 2 to 3 hours.

Cut into bars and serve cold or at room temperature.

# Chocolate-Dipped Strawberry Easter Eggs

Yields: 15 to 20 pieces | Prep time: 20 minutes | Cook time: n/a | Total time: 20 minutes

15 to 20 strawberries

1½ cups milk chocolate chips

1 tablespoon vegetable oil

4 tubes Cake Mate Writing Icing, in four different colors

Wash and dry each strawberry and remove any green stem or leaves. Line a cookie sheet with parchment paper. Melt chocolate chips in the microwave in 10-second intervals, stirring after each heating, until mostly melted. Stir in vegetable oil until well blended and smooth. Spear each berry with a fork and dip into the melted chocolate, covering ⅔ of the berry. Lay berries on the parchment paper. Once all strawberries have been covered, refrigerate for 30 minutes or until the chocolate hardens.

Decorate each berry with icing.

# Strawberry Carrot Dirt Cup

Yield: 12 Dirt Cups | Prep time: 40 minutes | Cook time: n/a | Total time: 40 minutes

- 1 (12-ounce) package orange candy melts
- 12 medium-large strawberries
- 2 (6-ounce) packages instant chocolate pudding
- 6 cups milk
- 12 (8-ounce) clear plastic cups
- 2 cups finely crushed Oreo crumbs

In a large microwave-safe bowl, melt orange candy according to package directions. Holding each strawberry by its green stem (making sure you don't miss any leaves), roll in candy melts so the entire red portion of the berry is covered. Place on waxed paper to set up. Drizzle extra orange candy melts on top of each dipped strawberry by pouring the leftover mixture into a small plastic bag and snipping off a small corner of the bag.

In a large bowl, mix together instant pudding and milk according to package directions. Evenly distribute pudding between 12 clear cups and let it set up, about 5 minutes. Sprinkle finely crushed Oreos on top of each cup of pudding, and place a strawberry "carrot" on top of each one.

# Frozen Creamy Jell-O

Serves: 6 to 8 | Prep time: 2 hours | Cook time: 15 minutes | Total time: 2 hours, 15 minutes

1 (8-ounce) can crushed pineapple with juice

½ cup granulated sugar

1 (3-ounce) package lime or orange Jell-O

1 cup heavy cream

1 cup sour cream

Line a loaf pan with waxed paper and set aside.

In a small pan over medium-high heat, bring pineapple and sugar to a full, rolling boil; remove from heat.

Stir in Jell-O and let cool.

In a separate large bowl, whip cream with an electric mixer on high speed until stiff peaks form. Fold in sour cream. And Jell-O mixture and whip again to combine well.

Pour mixture into prepared loaf pan, cover with foil and freeze. When ready to serve, turn out frozen Jell-O onto a cutting board and slice.

# TRADITIONS

## 6 Ways to Color Eggs

**1. Rice and Food Coloring.** This method is perfect for little kids because it is virtually mess free.

### Materials needed:

Long grain rice

Plastic bowls with lids

Food coloring

Hard-boiled eggs

**Directions:** Add ¼ cup rice to each bowl, followed by 6 generous drops food coloring of your choice. Cover each bowl with lid and shake vigorously.

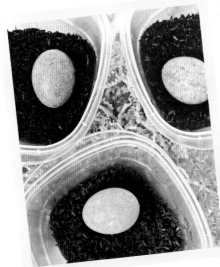

Place an egg in each bowl and cover with the rice. Replace lid and gently shake until egg is coated.

Remove egg and let dry on a paper towel.

**2. Chalkboard Paint.** This creative method lets you decorate plastic rather than real eggs. Once the plastic eggs are coated in chalkboard paint, kids can use chalk to write anything they want on their eggs. If they make a mistake, just wipe it off and write it again.

### Materials needed:

Plastic eggs

Chalkboard paint

Paint brush

Chalk

**Directions:** Paint each egg with 2 to 3 coats of chalkboard paint, allowing eggs to dry between coats.

Use chalk to decorate each egg: add names, doodle, draw hearts or flowers, and so on.

**3. Rubber-Band-Dyed Easter Eggs.** Wrapping eggs with rubber bands before dyeing them makes for a cool design. It's easier to wrap eggs with several rubber bands at once than to do it one at a time. This is activity is also better for kids who are a little older.

**Materials needed:**

Hard-boiled eggs

Rubber bands (10 to 12 per egg)

White vinegar

Food coloring

**Directions:** Make sure eggs have cooled completely and are very dry. Position 10 to 12 rubber bands around an egg. Rearrange the rubber bands so they interlock around the center of the egg and stay firmly in place.

Now arrange the bands in a netlike design around each egg. Set aside while preparing dye.

To prepare dye, in a large mug or plastic cup, mix ¾ cup warm water with 1 tablespoon white vinegar and 10 drops of your desired food coloring.

Submerge a rubber-band-wrapped egg into the dye. Allow the egg to sit for at least 5 minutes. The longer it stays there, the deeper the color will be. Remove the egg from the dye and let it air dry. Once dry, carefully remove rubber bands to reveal a nice streaked pattern.

**4. Electrical Tape Eggs.** This creative dyeing method will give you eggs with different colored stripes.

**Materials needed:**

Hard-boiled eggs

Electrical tape

Food coloring

White vinegar

**Directions:** Make sure eggs are dried and cooled completely. Cut electrical tape into 3-inch strips and wrap the strips around the hard-boiled eggs in any design you'd like.

To prepare dye, in a large mug or plastic cup, mix ¾ cup warm water with 1 tablespoon white vinegar and 10 drops of your desired food coloring.

Submerge a wrapped egg in the dye. Let it set a few minutes and then remove one strand of the electrical tape, and submerge egg in another color or the same one. Continue this process until you get your desired effect. You may even opt to leave a few stripes white.

5. **Marbled Eggs.** This one is probably best for older kids as it calls for carefully putting some fine cracks in the boiled eggs.

**Materials Needed:**

Hard-boiled eggs

Water

White vinegar

Food coloring

**Directions:** Tap a cooled, hard-boiled egg gently on a hard surface so it cracks a little, then roll the egg on the table so there are cracks all over the shell. Do not peel off any of the shell!

To prepare dye, in a large mug or plastic cup, mix ¾ cup warm water with 1 tablespoon white vinegar and 10 drops of your desired food coloring.

Dip the cracked egg into the prepared dye. Let soak until desired color is reached.

6. **Kool-Aid Eggs.** Your kids will get a kick out of this dyeing method, as the eggs will take on the color and scent of the powdered drink mix.

**Materials Needed:**

Hard-boiled eggs

Hot water

Kool-Aid packets (red, orange, blue, green, yellow, purple, and any other color/flavor you prefer)

**Directions:** In a large mug or 12-ounce cup, combine ⅔ cup water and 1 packet Kool-Aid until Kool-Aid is dissolved. Repeat with each packet of Kool-Aid. Submerge an egg in each cup and let it sit until it reaches the desired color.

# MAY

## *Recipes for a Mother's Day Brunch*

# Skillet-Sized Sweet Roll

Serves: 8 | Prep time: 20 minutes | Cook time: 20 minutes | Total time: 40 minutes

3 (12-ounce) cans refrigerated biscuits

⅓ cup butter, melted

1 cup brown sugar

1 (21-ounce) can cherry pie filling (or another favorite flavor)

2 ounces cream cheese, at room temperature

2 tablespoons butter, at room temperature

1 teaspoon vanilla extract

1 cup powdered sugar

2 teaspoons milk

Preheat oven to 350 degrees F. Grease a 10-inch oven-safe skillet. Place melted butter in a shallow bowl and brown sugar in a separate shallow bowl.

On a flat, clean surface, roll out all of the biscuits individually until they are pretty flat. Take each flattened biscuit and dip it in the melted butter (shaking off the excess) and then toss it in the brown sugar.

Place a small spoonful of cherry pie filling in the middle of each sugared biscuit and then roll it up. Place biscuits in a circle, starting in the center and working your way to the outside of prepared skillet to make a giant "roll." (Don't worry that it's messy; it will taste great!)

Bake 18 to 20 minutes, until roll starts to turn golden brown. Remove from oven and let it cool 5 minutes while preparing frosting.

For frosting: In a small bowl, mix together cream cheese, 2 tablespoons butter, vanilla, powdered sugar, and milk with an electric mixer until smooth.

Pour frosting over the top of the sweet roll and serve!

# Easy Lemon Berry Tarts

Yield: 24 tarts | Prep time: 5 minutes | Cook time: 7 minutes | Total time: 12 minutes

24 wonton wrappers

1 tablespoon unsalted butter, melted

¾ cup sweetened condensed milk

1 cup whipped cream or nondairy whipped topping, thawed

1 cup lemon fruit filling or lemon curd, such as Private Selection California Lemon Fruit Filling

24 raspberries

24 blueberries

24 blackberries

Powdered sugar for topping

Preheat oven to 375 degrees F.

Place 1 wonton wrapper in each cup of a nonstick muffin tin and lightly brush with melted butter.

Bake 7 minutes, or until wrappers begin to turn golden brown on the edges.

Whisk together sweetened condensed milk, whipped cream, and lemon filling.

Once wonton wrappers have cooled, spoon filling into wonton wrappers, and top each with 1 raspberry, 1 blueberry, and 1 blackberry.

Dust with powdered sugar and serve!

# Stuffed Cinnamon Sticks

Serves: 16 | Prep time: 15 minutes | Cook time: 20 minutes | Total time: 35 minutes

16 slices white bread

1 (8-ounce) brick cream cheese, at room temperature

¾ cup powdered sugar

1 cup granulated sugar

2 teaspoons ground cinnamon

½ cup Nutella

½ cup diced strawberries

½ cup blueberries

¾ cup butter, melted

Preheat oven to 350 degrees F.

Cut the crusts off each slice of bread and flatten bread with a rolling pin.

In a medium bowl, beat cream cheese and powdered sugar together with an electric mixer until smooth.

In another bowl, combine sugar and cinnamon and set aside.

Spread half the bread slices with 1 tablespoon Nutella each; spread the other half with the cream-cheese mixture. Top Nutella with diced strawberries; top the cream cheese mixture with fresh blueberries.

Roll up each slice tightly and dip in the butter, then roll in the sugar-cinnamon mixture.

Place seam-side down on an ungreased baking dish and bake 20 minutes, until golden brown.

# Blueberry Coffee Cake

Serves: 8 | Prep time: 20 minutes | Cook time: 30 minutes | Total time: 50 minutes

2 cups all-purpose flour

½ cup granulated sugar, plus 2 tablespoons for topping

4 teaspoons baking powder

½ teaspoon salt

1 large egg

¾ cup milk

3 tablespoons canola oil

1 (5.3-ounce) container vanilla yogurt

2¼ cups blueberries

¼ teaspoon ground cinnamon

⅛ teaspoon ground nutmeg

Preheat oven to 400 degrees F. Spray a 9-inch round baking dish with nonstick cooking spray and set aside.

In a large bowl, whisk together flour, ½ cup of the sugar, baking powder, and salt.

In a separate bowl, whisk together egg, milk, canola oil, and yogurt.

Stir together wet and dry ingredients until just combined.

Slowly fold in 1¾ cups of the blueberries, saving the last ½ cup for the top of the cake.

Pour batter into prepared baking sheet and top with remaining blueberries.

In a separate bowl, mix together remaining sugar, nutmeg, and cinnamon. Sprinkle over the unbaked cake.

Bake 25 to 30 minutes, until a toothpick inserted into the middle comes out clean.

# Berry Oatmeal Bake

Serves: 9 | Prep time: 15 minutes | Cook time: 35 minutes | Total time: 50 minutes

| | | | |
|---|---|---|---|
| 2 | cups rolled oats | 1 | tablespoon butter, melted |
| ½ | cup brown sugar | 1½ | cups vanilla almond milk |
| ½ | teaspoon baking soda | 1 | egg |
| ½ | teaspoon ground cinnamon | 2 | teaspoons vanilla extract |
| ½ | cup mini-chocolate chips | 1 | banana |
| 1½ | cups frozen berries | | |

Preheat oven to 375 degrees F. Grease a 9x13-inch pan.

In a large bowl, bowl, mix together oats, brown sugar, baking soda, cinnamon, and chocolate chips.

Fold frozen berries into dry mix. Spread dry mixture over bottom of prepared pan.

In a separate bowl, whisk together melted butter, almond milk, egg, and vanilla extract. Pour the mixture evenly over the oatmeal mixture.

Slice the banana into ¼-inch slices and spread over the top.

Bake 30 to 35 minutes, until top is nicely browned. Sprinkle with a little additional brown sugar and serve warm.

# Nutella-Stuffed French Toast

Serves: 4 | Prep time: 10 minutes | Cook time: 10 minutes | Total time: 20 minutes

4   eggs

½   cup heavy cream

¼   cup powdered sugar

8   slices Texas toast or thick white bread

8   tablespoons Nutella

Powdered sugar for topping

Maple syrup, optional

Preheat a nonstick skillet over medium-low heat.

In a bowl, whisk together the eggs, cream, and powdered sugar.

Take 2 slices of the Texas toast and spread 1 tablespoon of Nutella on each one.

Sandwich together and dip both sides in the custard mixture.

Cook each side until brown, about 3 to 4 minutes.

Remove from heat, dust with powdered sugar, and serve with maple syrup if desired.

# Cinnamon Breakfast Bites

Serves: 6 | Prep time: 10 minutes | Cook time: 15 minutes | Total time: 25 minutes

- 1⅓ cups all-purpose flour
- 1 cup Rice Krispies cereal, coarsely crushed
- 2 tablespoons granulated sugar
- 2 teaspoons baking powder
- ½ teaspoon salt
- ¼ cup butter-flavored shortening
- ½ cup milk
- 1½ teaspoons ground cinnamon
- ⅔ cup granulated sugar
- ⅓ cup butter, melted

Preheat oven to 420 degrees F. Spray an 8x8-inch baking pan with nonstick cooking spray.

In a mixing bowl, combine the flour, crushed cereal, 2 tablespoons sugar, baking powder, and salt. Cut in the shortening until mixture resembles coarse crumbs.

Stir in milk just until moistened. (The mixture should be kind of dry, but if it seems too crumbly, add an extra teaspoon of milk so it's all barely moistened.) Shape dough into 1-inch balls.

In a small bowl combine the cinnamon and ⅔ cup sugar. Dip each ball into butter, then roll into cinnamon-sugar mixture. Arrange dough balls in a single layer in prepared pan and bake 15 to 17 minutes.

# Apple Walnut Pull-Apart Bread

Serves: 6 | Prep time: 1 hour, 15 minutes | Cook time: 35 minutes | Total time: 1 hour, 50 minutes

12 frozen dinner rolls, thawed

2 Granny Smith apples, chopped

⅓ cup brown sugar

½ cup walnuts, finely chopped

½ teaspoon ground cinnamon

2 tablespoons butter, melted

Preheat oven to 350 degrees F. Spray a 9×5-inch loaf pan with nonstick cooking spray.

Mix together the chopped apples, brown sugar, walnuts, and cinnamon until well combined.

Using a pair of clean kitchen scissors, cut each roll into thirds.

Place 12 small roll pieces in the bottom of the loaf pan. Drizzle about a third of the melted butter on top of the roll pieces. Then top with a third of the apple mixture. Repeat 2 more times, until all ingredients have been used.

Let rise for about an hour, or until rolls have doubled in size.

Bake 30 to 35 minutes, until tops are golden brown and the middle rolls are done.

# Turkey Bacon Egg Muffin Cups

Serves: 12 | Prep time: 10 minutes | Cook time: 30 minutes | Total time: 40 minutes

| | | |
|---|---|---|
| 12 | slices Jennie-O Turkey Bacon | Salt and pepper, to taste |
| 6 | slices wheat bread | ½ cup shredded cheddar cheese |
| 12 | eggs | ¼ cup sliced green onion |

Preheat oven to 375 degrees F. Spray a muffin tin with nonstick cooking spray.

Place a piece of turkey bacon around the inside edge of each muffin cup.

Using a small circle cookie cutter, cut out 12 circles of bread and place one circle in the bottom of each muffin cup.

Crack an egg in each muffin cup on top of the bread. Season with salt and pepper, add a sprinkle of cheddar cheese, and garnish with sliced green onion.

Bake 30 minutes, or until egg is set up in the middle.

# Cinnamon Roll French Bread Bake

Serves: 8 | Prep time: 15 minutes | Cook time: 25 minutes | Total time: 40 minutes

1 to 2 loaves French bread
5 eggs
¾ cup whole milk
2 teaspoons vanilla extract

1 tablespoon ground cinnamon, divided
2 teaspoons ground nutmeg
½ cup brown sugar
1 cup cream cheese frosting or vanilla frosting, melted

Preheat oven to 350 degrees F. Grease a 9x13-inch baking pan.

Slice the French bread into ½- to ⅓-inch slices and place one layer of bread in prepared pan.

In a large bowl, whisk together eggs, whole milk, vanilla, ½ tablespoon cinnamon, and nutmeg until well combined.

Pour half of the liquid mixture over the slices of bread.

Place another layer of the sliced bread on top of that. Pour the rest of the liquid mixture over the other slices of bread.

Sprinkle brown sugar and remaining cinnamon on top and place in the preheated oven. Bake 25 minutes, or until all the liquid is absorbed and baked into the bread.

Remove from oven and let cool for about 5 minutes, and then spoon melted cream cheese frosting on top.

Serve warm and enjoy!

# Breakfast Tacos

Serves: 8 | Prep time: 25 minutes | Cook time: n/a | Total time: 25 minutes

4 red potatoes, diced

1 green pepper, diced

1 tablespoon extra-virgin olive oil

4 eggs

1 tablespoon milk

Salt and pepper to taste

8 taco-sized corn or flour tortillas

1 cup refried beans

4 to 6 strips bacon, cooked crisp and crumbled

In a large skillet over medium heat, cook the diced potatoes and peppers in the vegetable oil until completely cooked through and potatoes are soft.

In a separate pan over medium heat whisk together milk and eggs and scramble them in pan until done. Season with salt and pepper to taste.

Spread a spoonful of refried beans in center of each tortilla.

Top with eggs, potatoes and peppers, cheese, and bacon.

Fold tortillas in half, forming tacos. Best if served warm, immediately, but can be stored in airtight container in refrigerator for up to 2 days.

# TRADITIONS

*Homemade Gifts for Mom*

## Cookbook Stand

This cookbook stand costs only a few dollars to make, and you can have a hardware store do the cutting for you if you don't have your own saw. Pair it with your favorite cookbook and you have the perfect homemade gift for Mom, Grandma, or a friend.

### Materials needed:

- 1-inch by 12-inch by 1-inch board
- 1 (1-inch) narrow utility hinge
- 2-inch brad nails or screws
- Sandpaper
- Wood filler
- Stain or paint
- 2 small eye hooks or ½-inch pan head screws
- 8 inches string

**Step 1.** Cut 2 (1-inch wide) pieces of wood from the bottom of the board.

**Step 2.** Cut a 1½x6-inch piece of wood from the board to make the kickstand.

**Step 3.** Sand all of the pieces as necessary.

**Step 4.** Stack the two 1-inch-wide pieces, making a lip at the bottom of your cookbook stand. Apply wood glue to the joining faces and secure with 2-inch brad nails or screws. Once the glue is dry, round the bottom outer corners with sandpaper or a sander.

**Step 3.** Remove any excess glue, apply wood filler to holes, cracks, and blemishes and allow to dry. Sand the wood filler and holder until smooth, finishing with 120–150 grit sandpaper. Paint or stain the holder and kickstand. Allow to dry.

### Homemade Lotion Bars

4.5 ounces beeswax

4 ounces shea butter

4 ounces coconut oil

Combine all ingredients in a double boiler. Melt and stir until ingredients are completely mixed together. Pour your lotion into molds.

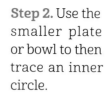

You can use all kinds of materials for molds such as plastic, metal, ice cube trays, or cupcake pans.

Allow lotion to completely cool before popping out and using. For ease in removing from mold, place in freezer for 30 minutes and then remove.

### Easy Monogrammed Doormat

1 sisal or kempf doormat

2 plates or bowls, one slightly smaller than the other

1 permanent marking pen, such as a Sharpie

Letter template

Black acrylic craft paint, plus a small brush

Measuring tape

**Step 1.** Trace the larger circle with a permanent marker directly onto doormat.

**Step 2.** Use the smaller plate or bowl to then trace an inner circle.

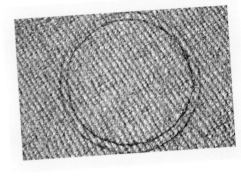

**Step 3.** Create a stencil of the first letter of your mom's last name by printing the letter in the font of your choice on your computer. Enlarge the image on a copier so it fits within the circle. Cut out the letter. Measure the center of the circle and place the stencil in the correct spot. Trace the letter with a permanent marker.

**Step 4.** Using black craft paint and a small brush, fill in the circle and monogram

# JUNE

## *Dad's Favorite Grilling Recipes*

# Chipotle Lime Chicken

Serves: 4 to 6 | Prep time: 2 hours, 20 minutes | Cook time: 20 minutes | Total time: 2 hours, 40 minutes

| | | | |
|---|---|---|---|
| 2 | tablespoons olive oil | 2 | teaspoons minced garlic |
| ½ | cup lime juice | 3 | tablespoons honey |
| ¼ | cup low-sodium soy sauce | | Salt to taste |
| ¼ | cup fresh chopped cilantro | 4 to 6 | boneless, skinless chicken breasts |
| 2 | teaspoons chipotle chili powder | 2 | limes for garnish |

In a medium bowl, whisk together the olive oil, lime juice, soy sauce, cilantro, chipotle chili powder, minced garlic, honey, and salt until well combined.

Set ½ cup of the marinade aside.

Transfer remaining marinade to a large zipper-top bag, add chicken breasts, seal, and shake or massage the bag to ensure the chicken is well coated.

Refrigerate 2 to 6 hours. Remove chicken from bag and discard used marinade.

Grill chicken breasts over medium-high heat, basting chicken with the ½ cup reserved marinade.

Grill until the chicken is done all the way through and the outsides are dark golden brown. A meat thermometer should register 165 degrees F.

Serve with fresh lime and enjoy!

# Grilled Steak

Serves: 4 | Prep time: 10 minutes | Cook time: 10 minutes | Total time: 20 minutes

¼ cup honey

¼ cup low-sodium soy sauce

2 tablespoons lemon juice

½ teaspoon ground ginger

1 teaspoon minced garlic

2 pounds flank or skirt steak, sliced about ½-inch thick

In a medium bowl, whisk together honey, soy sauce, lemon juice, ginger, and garlic. Transfer to a large zipper-top bag, add steak strips, seal, and shake or massage the bag to ensure the steak is well coated.

Marinate at least 30 minutes or up to overnight in the refrigerator. Remove steak strips from bag and discard marinade.

Grill over medium heat until steak pieces reach desired doneness.

# Garlic Parmesan Herb Salmon

Serves 4 to 5 | Prep time: 15 minutes | Cook time: 15 minutes | Total time: 30 minutes

4 to 5 (5-ounce) salmon fillets

2 tablespoons olive oil

1 tablespoon Italian seasoning

1 teaspoon minced garlic

½ teaspoon black pepper

½ cup grated Parmesan cheese

Heat grill to medium-low heat, and spray racks with nonstick cooking spray.

In a bowl, combine olive oil, Italian seasoning, garlic, pepper, and Parmesan cheese until fully incorporated.

Dip salmon into the mixture and place on hot grill, flipping every 3 minutes for about 15 minutes, or until the fish is cooked through and flakes easily with a fork. Baste the salmon as you go with the garlic Parmesan mixture to keep the fish moist and full of flavor.

# Grilled Lemon Chicken

Serves: 4 | Prep time: 8 minutes | Cook time: 12 minutes | Total time: 20 minutes

| | |
|---|---|
| 4 boneless, skinless chicken breasts | 2 cloves garlic, minced |
| ½ cup fresh lemon juice | ½ teaspoon ground ginger |
| ¼ cup soy sauce | ½ teaspoon onion powder |
| ¼ cup olive oil | ¼ teaspoon red pepper flakes |

In a medium bowl, whisk together lemon juice, soy sauce, olive oil, garlic, ginger, onion powder, and red pepper flakes.

Transfer marinade to a large zipper-top bag, add chicken breasts, seal, and shake or massage the bag to ensure the chicken is well coated.

Place bag in the refrigerator and let chicken marinate 4 to 8 hours.

Remove chicken from bag and discard marinade.

Place chicken on grill over medium-high heat, cooking about 5 to 6 minutes on each side, or until the internal temperature registers 165 degrees F. on a meat thermometer.

# Guacamole Bacon Burgers

Serves: 6 | Prep time: 10 minutes | Cook time: 10 minutes | Total time: 20 minutes

1½  pounds ground beef

Garlic powder, to taste

Seasoning salt, to taste

12  slices bacon, cooked crisp

1½  cups guacamole, fresh or store-bought

6  slices pepper Jack cheese

6  hamburger buns

In a large bowl, mix together ground beef, garlic powder, and seasoning salt and then shape into patties.

Grill burgers on a hot grill 5 to 7 minutes on each side.

Place burgers on buns and top each with 2 slices bacon, ¼ cup guacamole, a slice of cheese, and any other desired toppings.

# Asian Marinated Pork

Serves: 6 | Prep time: 4 hours | Cook time: 10 minutes | Total time: 4 hours, 10 minutes

1  cup soy sauce

½  cup brown sugar

2  teaspoons minced garlic

1  teaspoon ground ginger

1  tablespoon ground cumin

1  teaspoon chili powder

6  boneless pork chops

In a small bowl, whisk together soy sauce, brown sugar, garlic, ginger, cumin, and chili powder. Transfer marinade to a large zipper-top bag and add pork chops. Seal bag and place in the refrigerator at least 4 hours. After marinating, preheat a grill or skillet to medium-high heat. Place pork chops on preheated grill or skillet and cook 5 to 7 minutes per side until internal temperature registers 145 degrees F. on a meat thermometer.

# Loaded Hot Dogs

Serves: 8 | Prep time: 15 minutes | Cook time: n/a | Total time: 15 minutes

8　hot dogs, grilled

8　hot dog buns

1　cup shredded Monterey Jack cheese

8　slices of bacon, cooked crisp

1　cup Quick Pico de Gallo

1　avocado, sliced thin

1　jalapeño, sliced thin

　　Chipotle mayo for topping

In each hot dog bun, sprinkle an even amount of shredded cheese.

Top with a hot dog, then tuck a piece of bacon in the bun next to each dog.

Top each dog with pico de gallo, 1 to 2 slices avocado, jalapeño slices, and a drizzle of chipotle mayo.
Serve warm.

## Quick Pico de Gallo

4　firm Roma tomatoes, diced

1　medium onion, diced

1　jalapeño pepper, diced (see note)

4　tablespoons diced cilantro

　　Juice of 2 limes

1　teaspoon minced garlic

Combine all ingredients in a small bowl and refrigerate 2 hours before serving.

*Note:* For mild pico, discard jalapeño seeds before dicing it.

# Bonsai Burgers

Serves: 4 | Prep time: 35 minutes | Cook time: 15 minutes | Total time: 50 minutes

| | |
|---|---|
| 1⅓ pounds ground beef | 4 hamburger buns with sesame seeds |
| 2 cups teriyaki sauce, divided | 4 tablespoons mayonnaise |
| 4 pineapple rings | 4 slices tomatoes |
| 4 slices cheddar cheese | 1 cup shredded lettuce |

Form ground beef into 4 equal-sized patties.

Pour 1 cup of the teriyaki sauce in a shallow bowl, add hamburger patties, spooning sauce over the top to cover, and let marinate in sauce for at least 30 minutes.

Pour remaining cup teriyaki sauce in a separate shallow bowl and let pineapple rings marinate at the same time.

Remove hamburger patties from teriyaki sauce and grill on high heat until you patties desired doneness.

Melt cheese on top of hamburgers while still on the grill.

Grill pineapple rings on medium heat for 1 minute on each side.

Spread ½ tablespoon of mayonnaise on each half of each hamburger bun. Place tomato slices on the bottom buns and top with hamburger patties. On top of each hamburger patty, place a pineapple ring and shredded lettuce. Cover with top half of hamburger bun.

Serve with extra teriyaki sauce.

# Grilled Tuscan Pork Chops

Serves: 4 to 6 | Prep time: 6 hours, 5 minutes | Cook time: 8 to 10 minutes | Total time: 6 hours, 15 minutes

4 to 6 (¾-inch thick) pork rib chops

1 (16-ounce) bottle zesty Italian salad dressing

¼ cup balsamic vinegar

2 tablespoons honey

1 teaspoon dried rosemary

½ teaspoon freshly ground black pepper

Place the pork chops in a large zipper-top bag and pour in the whole bottle of salad dressing. Seal the bag, removing the excess air, and shake to coat the chops well.

Refrigerate the chops and let them marinate 4 to 6 hours. Remove the chops from the bag and shake off the excess marinade. Set them aside on a platter.

Pour the marinade into a small sauce pan and add the balsamic vinegar, honey, rosemary, and black pepper. Bring the mixture to a slight boil over medium heat. Boil the liquid gently for five minutes, then remove from the heat. This kills any germs that were hanging out in the marinade and reduces the marinade to a sauce perfect for drizzling over grilled chops.

Cook chops on a hot grill for 3 to 4 minutes on each side, until internal temperature registers 145 degrees F. on a meat thermometer.

# Grilled Huli Huli Chicken

Serves: 5 to 6 | Prep time: 10 minutes | Cook time: 15 minutes | Total time: 25 minutes

½ cup pineapple juice

½ cup brown sugar

⅓ cup ketchup

⅓ cup soy sauce

¼ teaspoon ground ginger

2 cloves garlic, minced

6 boneless, skinless chicken breasts or thighs

In a small bowl, whisk together pineapple juice, brown sugar, ketchup, soy sauce, ginger, and garlic. Transfer marinade to a large zipper-top plastic bag and add chicken. Seal bag and place in the refrigerator for at least 8 hours or overnight.

Remove bag from fridge; drain and discard marinade from chicken.

Grill chicken over medium-high heat 6 to 8 minutes on each side, or until internal temperature of chicken registers 165 degrees F. on a meat thermometer.

# TRADITIONS

## A Summer Bucket List

At the beginning of each summer, we hang a large piece of paper on our wall and write down all the things we want to do that summer to make the most of every day! You could aim to do a couple of things each week or even one a day to have an amazing summer full of fun memories.

1. **Go to a drive-in movie**
2. **Make homemade popsicles**
3. **Play croquet**
4. **Go bowling**
5. **Go swimming**
6. **Make s'mores**
7. **Play in the sprinklers**
8. **Have a read-a-thon**
9. **Have a picnic**
10. **Watch fireworks**
11. **Go to a parade**
12. **Play miniature golf**
13. **Go to a farmer's market**
14. **Get snow cones**
15. **Make homemade ice cream**
16. **Have a lemonade stand**
17. **Make homemade pizza**
18. **Have a BBQ with friends**
19. **Go camping**
20. **Go on a hike**
21. **Have a movie marathon**

22. Plant something (garden, flowers)

23. Have a karaoke night

24. Go to the beach

25. Go to a baseball game

26. Visit a splash pad

27. Go to a park we have never been to

28. Visit a museum

29. Go to an outdoor concert

30. Have a family game night

31. Make cookies

32. Get a library card and read a new book each month

33. Make root beer floats

34. Do a service project

35. Hold a puppet show

36. Tie-dye T-shirts

37. Build a big blanket fort

38. Go to a rodeo

39. Play on a slip-and-slide

40. Go fishing

41. Decorate a cake

42. Make your own obstacle course

43. Let the kids plan and make dinner

44. Watch the sunrise

45. Do a puzzle

46. Camp in the backyard

47. Go on a scavenger hunt

48. Go to the zoo

49. Make a time capsule

50. Go rollerblading

# JULY

*Recipes for a Patriotic Picnic*

# Red, White, and Blue Jell-O

Serves: 16 | Prep time: 6 hours, 15 minutes | Cook time: n/a | Total time: 6 hours, 15 minutes

1 (6-ounce) box red Jell-O

1 (6-ounce) box blue Jell-O

1 (14-ounce) can sweetened condensed milk

2 (1-ounce) envelopes Knox unflavored gelatin

Water

For each flavor, dissolve one box Jell-O in 2 cups boiling water. Pour each flavor in a separate 9x13-inch pan and chill at least 3 hours, or overnight.

After chilling the flavors, cut them into small squares. Gently toss both colors of Jell-O squares into a new 9×13-inch pan.

In a separate bowl, sprinkle 2 envelopes unflavored gelatin into ½ cup cold water. Let the gelatin expand in the water for a few minutes, then add 1½ cups boiling water and whisk together until the unflavored gelatin dissolves.

Whisk in the can of sweetened condensed milk, stirring well to combine. Let cool to room temperature.

Once the milk mixture has cooled, pour over Jell-O squares in the 9×13-inch pan. Chill for a few hours until set up. Cut into blocks or use cookie cutters to cut pieces into shapes and serve.

# Patriotic Popcorn

Serves: 8 | Prep time: 15 minutes | Cook time: n/a | Total time: 15 minutes

2 (2.75-ounce) bags kettle corn

2 cups white chocolate chips

2 cups red, white, and blue M&M's Chocolate Candies

Red, white, and blue sprinkles

Cover a baking sheet with waxed paper.

Pop kettle corn in microwave according to package directions and spread out on prepared baking sheet. Remove any unpopped kernels.

Place white chocolate chips in a large zipper-top bag and microwave on high power in 30-second intervals, squeezing after each interval until chocolate is smooth and melted.

Once the white chocolate chips are melted, cut a small corner off the bottom of the bag and drizzle melted white chocolate over popcorn.

Top with M&M's and sprinkles.

Let chocolate set up and serve.

# Patriotic Berry Trifle

Serves: 10 to 12 | Prep time: 25 minutes | Cook time: n/a | Total time: 25 minutes

¼ plus ⅔ cups granulated sugar

¼ cup fresh lemon juice

¼ cup water

¼ teaspoon almond extract

2 (8-ounce) bricks cream cheese, at room temperature

1 prepared angel food cake, cut into 1-inch slices

2 cups heavy cream

2 pints blueberries

2 pints strawberries, sliced

In a small saucepan over medium-high heat, stir ¼ cup sugar, lemon juice, and water until the sugar dissolves completely. Remove from heat and stir in the almond extract.

Brush both sides of each slice of cake with the syrup. Cut the slices into 1-inch cubes.

Beat the remaining ⅔ cup sugar with the cream cheese in a stand mixer on medium speed until smooth and light. Add the cream and beat on medium-high speed until mixture is smooth and forms soft peaks.

Arrange half of the cake cubes in the bottom of a trifle dish or large glass bowl. Sprinkle evenly with a layer of blueberries. Dollop half of the cream mixture over the blueberries and gently spread. Top with a layer of strawberries. Layer the remaining cake cubes on top of the strawberries, then sprinkle with more blueberries and top with the remaining cream mixture. Finish with the remaining strawberries and blueberries until the top is covered. Cover and refrigerate 1 hour, then serve.

Alternatively, you could make 10 to 12 individual servings in clear plastic or glass cups.

# Layered Cobb Salad

Serves: 12 | Prep time: 35 minutes | Cook time: n/a | Total time: 35 minutes

1 head iceberg lettuce, roughly chopped

4 Roma tomatoes, diced

1 red onion, minced

2 (15-ounce) cans corn, drained

12 hard-boiled eggs, peeled and diced

12 pieces bacon, cooked crisp and crumbled

4 avocados, diced

1 to 2 cups shredded cheddar cheese

Salad dressing of your choice

In a large glass bowl or trifle dish, layer ingredients in the order listed.
Serve with your favorite salad dressing.

# Fourth of July Chocolate Firecrackers

Serves: 8 | Prep time: 5 minutes | Cook time: n/a | Total time: 5 minutes

1 box Hostess Ho Hos

1 can or batch of your favorite frosting, tinted red

1 can or batch of your favorite frosting, tinted blue

Firework-themed crafting wire (see picture)

Put each color frosting in a separate zipper-top bag, seal bag, and snip off a corner to make a piping bag.

On a paper plate, pipe a quarter-sized blob of frosting and secure a Ho Ho to the plate as shown in picture. Use the piping bags to pipe on designs, stars, or the words "Happy 4th" in colors of your choice.

Pipe a few circles of either color frosting on top of each Ho Ho and then place the firework-themed crafting wire in the top of Ho Ho, using the frosting to secure it.

# Fruity Party Punch

Serves: 40 to 50 | Prep time: 5 minutes | Cook time: n/a | Total time: 5 minutes

1 (2 liter) bottle red fruit punch drink

1 (2 liter) bottle ginger ale

1 (46 ounce) can unsweetened pineapple juice

½ gallon orange sherbet

Ice

In a large punch bowl (or other large bowl), mix together the fruit punch, ginger ale, and pineapple juice.

Add scoops of sherbet to the punch bowl using an ice cream scoop.

After just a couple of minutes, the sherbet will start to melt. Using a large spoon or whisk, mix until the sherbet is completely incorporated into the liquid.

Add some ice and serve!

# Fresh Bruschetta

Serves: 12 | Prep time: 20 minutes | Cook time: n/a | Total time: 20 minutes

3 cups diced tomatoes, such as a mixture of Roma, cherry, and grape tomatoes

2 teaspoons minced garlic

2 tablespoons olive oil

¼ cup grated Parmesan cheese

4 tablespoons freshly chopped basil

2 tablespoons balsamic vinegar

Salt and pepper to taste

1 baguette

In a large bowl, mix together tomatoes, garlic, olive oil, Parmesan cheese, basil, and balsamic vinegar. Add salt and pepper to taste. Cover bowl, place in the fridge, and let the flavors meld for at least 15 to 30 minutes.

Cut baguette in ½-inch slices. Top with a scoop of tomato mixture and serve.

# Spaghetti Salad

Serves: 15 | Prep time: 20 minutes | Cook time: 8 minutes | Total time: 28 minutes

1 pound thin spaghetti, broken into 3- to 4-inch pieces

3 Roma tomatoes, diced

1 medium zucchini, diced

1 medium yellow squash, diced

1 green pepper, diced

1 red pepper, diced

1 red onion, diced

1 cucumber, diced

2 (2.25-ounce) cans sliced olives, drained

8 ounces cheddar cheese, cut into small cubes

1 (16-ounce) bottle Italian dressing

¼ cup grated Parmesan cheese

1 teaspoon paprika

¼ teaspoon garlic powder

1 teaspoon Salad Supreme or Johnny's Seasoning (optional)

Cook spaghetti pieces according to package directions, then rinse in cold water and drain. Set aside and let cool.

Place tomatoes, zucchini, squash, peppers, onion, cucumber, olives, and cheese cubes in a large bowl. Add cooled spaghetti noodles and mix well.

In a small bowl, mix together Italian dressing, Parmesan cheese, paprika, and garlic powder. Pour on top of the spaghetti and vegetables and mix until completely combined. Sprinkle the top with Salad Supreme or Johnny's Seasoning if desired.

Chill in refrigerator at least 2 hours before serving.

# Grilled Island Chicken Kebabs

Serves: 6 | Prep time: 20 minutes, plus marinade time | Cook time: 16 minutes | Total time: 36 minutes

2 to 4 boneless, skinless chicken breasts, cut into bite-sized pieces

⅓ cup vegetable oil

¼ cup fresh lemon juice

2 tablespoons soy sauce

1 clove garlic, finely minced

½ teaspoon dried oregano

¼ teaspoon salt

¼ teaspoon freshly ground black pepper

1 large red onion, cut into chunks

1 large green pepper, cut into chunks

1 pineapple, peeled, cored, and cut into large chunks

Combine vegetable oil, lemon juice, soy sauce, garlic, oregano, salt, and pepper in a small bowl and then transfer to a large, zipper-top bag. Place chicken in bag, seal, and massage bag to ensure all pieces are covered. Place chicken in refrigerator and let marinate at least 3 hours or up to overnight.

If using wooden skewers, let your skewers soak in water 1 hour before using. This helps to prevent burning. Thread chicken, onions, peppers, and pineapple on skewers until you run out of ingredients.

Heat grill to medium and cook skewers 7 to 8 minutes per side, or until chicken is no longer pink in the middle (if using a meat thermometer, make sure it registers 165 degrees F).

Remove from grill and serve!

# Ham and Swiss Sliders

Serves: 24 | Prep time: 15 minutes | Cook time: 20 minutes: | Total time: 35 minutes

24 King's Hawaiian Rolls

½ cup butter, melted

½ yellow onion, minced

1½ tablespoons Dijon mustard

1½ tablespoons poppy seeds

1 teaspoon Worcestershire sauce

8 slices Swiss deli cheese, cut into fourths

28 slices deli ham

Preheat oven to 325 degrees F.

Slice rolls in half, keeping tops and bottoms together.

In a small bowl whisk together melted butter, onion, mustard, poppy seeds, and Worcestershire sauce.

Brush the mixture evenly on both the top and bottom halves of each roll.

On the bottom half of each roll, top the mustard mixture with a small slice of Swiss cheese and 2 slices ham.

Places rolls on a large baking sheet, cover with foil, and bake 15 to 20 minutes, or until cheese is melted.

Remove from oven, separate rolls, and serve.

# TRADITIONS

## *S'mores and Campouts*

We love summer, campouts, starry nights, and lots of s'mores. Here are 12 s'mores variations to try out around the campfire this summer.

1. **Peanut Butter and Banana:** graham crackers, banana slices, peanut butter, and marshmallows

2. **Churro:** cinnamon graham crackers, butterscotch chips, white chocolate, and marshmallows

3. **Mint Chocolate:** graham crackers, Andes mints (this would be good with chocolate graham crackers, too), and marshmallows

4. **Caramel Apple:** cinnamon graham crackers, green apples, ROLOS, and marshmallows

5. **Samoas:** graham crackers, caramel, coconut flakes, chocolate, and marshmallows

6. **Strawberry:** graham crackers, chocolate, sliced strawberries, and marshmallows

7. **Nutella:** graham crackers, Nutella, and marshmallows

8. **Reese's:** graham crackers, Reese's peanut butter cups, and marshmallows

9. **Salted Caramel:** graham crackers, dark chocolate, caramel, a sprinkle of sea salt, and marshmallows

10. **Cookie Butter:** graham crackers, cookie butter, and marshmallows

11. **Chocolate Chip Cookie:** chocolate chip cookies, chocolate, and marshmallows

12. **Sweet and Salty:** graham crackers, chocolate, pretzels, and marshmallows

Add these s'mores to our 10 camping hacks and your summer will be one to remember!

# 10 Camping Hacks

1. **DIY Fire Starter:** Stuff dryer lint (make sure it comes from cotton fabrics, not synthetic) into a toilet-paper roll. Roll the cardboard in newspaper and tuck in the ends.

2. **Repurpose Condiment Bottles:** Clean out a ketchup bottle to use as a pancake dispenser. That will save you from a few messes!

3. **DIY Water-Resistant Matchbox:** Fill a small mason jar with matches. Glue a small round of sandpaper to the inside top of the lid.

4. **Foam Floor Tiles for Tents:** Use foam tiles (that you would find in the children's section of any superstore) and place them interlocked on the bottom of your tent.

5. **Hanging Organizer:** Clear off your tables and have more room to eat or play games by hanging items like sunscreen, bug spray, and other essentials in an inexpensive hanging shoe organizer.

6. **DIY Lantern:** Fill a water jug with water, and place a headlamp around it with the light facing in. Turn on the headlamp whenever you need some extra light around the campground (for a fraction of the price of a lantern!).

7. **Use Frozen Water Jugs in Coolers:** Forget the ice! Use frozen water jugs in coolers. It's less of a mess, and you can drink it when it has melted!

8. **DIY Garbage Can:** Somehow, the "tie the bag to the tree" or "hang it off the side of the table" trick just always ends up in spilled garbage for our family! Use a pop-up hamper from the dollar store and line it with a trash bag for the perfect portable garbage can.

9. **Soap Hack:** We used to go camping with our grandparents and cousins every summer, and my grandma always used this trick for keeping soap off the ground! Just place a bar of soap (or soap pieces) in the sock end of some pantyhose and tie it around the water spout (or wherever you need one). You'll never lose the soap, but it will still clean your hands through the pantyhose.

10. **DIY Mini Medicine Cabinet:** Instead of packing a ton of medicine bottles for just a couple days of camping, use a pillbox to store medicine. Label the top of each lid with the type of medicine found inside.

# AUGUST

## Recipes to Beat the Heat with Ingredients Fresh from the Garden

# No-Bake Summer Fruit Pizza

Serves: 8 | Prep time: 20 minutes | Cook time: n/a | Total time: 20 minutes

2½ cups crushed graham crackers

½ cup sweetened condensed milk

1 teaspoon vanilla

1 (8-ounce) brick cream cheese, at room temperature

½ cup plain Greek yogurt

½ cup powdered sugar

10 strawberries, diced

½ cup fresh blueberries

⅓ cup sweetened flaked coconut

Combine the crushed graham crackers, sweetened condensed milk, and vanilla until well combined. Spread the mixture out on a pizza pan (you can also use a 9x13-inch baking dish).

In a separate bowl, with an electric mixer, combine cream cheese, Greek yogurt, and powdered sugar until smooth.

Spread this mixture over the graham cracker crust, leaving a little graham cracker crust showing around the edges.

Decorate pizza with strawberries, blueberries, and coconut. Dust with powdered sugar to finish.

# Frozen Lemonade

Serves: 4 | Prep time: 10 minutes | Cook time: n/a | Total time: 10 minutes

1   lemon, thinly sliced

1   cup granulated sugar

¾   cup cold water

¾   cup lemon lime soda

⅔   cup lemon juice

2 to 3   cups ice

In a large bowl, mash together lemon slices and sugar with a spoon.

Stir in water, soda, and lemon juice and let mixture rest 5 minutes, stirring occasionally.

In a blender, puree lemon juice mixture and ice until smooth. Use more ice for a thicker drink.

Pour into 4 glasses and serve.

# Dole Whips

Serves: 3 | Prep time: 10 minutes | Cook time: n/a | Total time: 10 minutes

1 (16-ounce) bag frozen pineapple chunks, thawed slightly

4 cups vanilla ice cream

1 teaspoon lime juice

1 teaspoon lemon juice

1½ cups pineapple juice

Puree slightly thawed frozen pineapple in a blender. To that, add the ice cream, lime juice, lemon juice, and ¾ cup of the pineapple juice. Blend together until it is well mixed.

Freeze the mixture for about 2 hours to set up.

Scoop into glasses or bowls and pour the remaining pineapple juice over each serving.

# Mango Berry Salad

Serves: 4 to 6 | Prep time: 10 minutes | Cook time: n/a | Total time: 10 minutes

1 (5-ounce) bag spring mix salad

1 cup fresh blueberries

2 cups fresh diced strawberries

3 mangoes, peeled and cubed, divided

½ cup sliced almonds

1 (8-ounce) carton vanilla Greek yogurt

1 tablespoon lemon juice

1 teaspoon honey

Pinch salt

In a large bowl, toss the spring mix, blueberries, strawberries, and 2 mangoes together. Top with sliced almonds.

In a blender (or food processor) mix together yogurt, lemon juice, remaining mango, honey, and salt. Blend until smooth, then pour over salad (or serve on the side).

# Strawberry Fluff Salad

Serves: 10 | Prep time: 6 hours | Cook time: 4 minutes | Total time: 6 hours, 4 minutes

- 1 (4.6-ounce) package cook-and-serve vanilla pudding
- 1 (6-ounce) package strawberry Jell-O
- 2 cups water
- 1 (16-ounce) tub nondairy whipped topping
- ½ (10.5-ounce) bag mini-marshmallows
- 2 cups chopped strawberries
- 2 to 3 bananas, sliced (optional)

In a large saucepan, mix together pudding, Jell-O, and water over medium heat until it boils, stirring regularly.

Remove from heat and pour into a large mixing bowl. Cover with plastic wrap.

Refrigerate until mixture has thickened, about 6 hours or overnight. Once thick, remove from refrigerator and beat with a hand mixer until creamy.

Fold in whipped topping, marshmallows, and fruit, except bananas, if using. Chill 1 hour before serving. If using bananas, fold in right before serving so they don't turn brown in the refrigerator.

# Cookies-and-Cream Fudge Popsicles

Serves: 10 | Prep time: 15 minutes | Freezer time: 4 hours | Total time: 4 hours, 15 minutes

1 (3.4-ounce) box instant chocolate pudding

2 cups milk

¾ cup heavy cream

15 Oreo Cookies

Prepare pudding according to package directions, using the 2 cups milk listed in the ingredients. Set aside.

Pour the cream into a bowl and beat with an electric mixer until stiff peaks form. Add to chocolate pudding and fold to combine.

Place the cookies in a large, zipper-top bag, seal bag, and crush cookies into chunks. Add to the pudding mixture and fold to combine.

Pour pudding mixture into popsicle molds and place the popsicles in the freezer until frozen solid, about 4 hours or up to overnight.

# Homemade Fresh Peach Milkshakes

Serves: 4 | Prep time: 5 minutes | Cook time: n/a | Total time: 5 minutes

3 medium-sized peaches, peeled and sliced

4 cups vanilla ice cream

1 cup milk

1 teaspoon vanilla extract

Combine all ingredients in a blender and blend until smooth. Serve and enjoy!

# Raspberry Fruit Dip

Serves: 4 to 6 | Prep time: 5 minutes | Cook time: n/a | Total time: 5 minutes

1 (8-ounce) brick cream cheese, softened

1 cup raspberries, fresh or frozen

1 teaspoon lemon juice

½ teaspoon ground cinnamon

¾ cup powdered sugar

In a small bowl, mix together all ingredients with an electric hand mixer. Serve with your favorite fruit or graham crackers.

Tastes great chilled or eaten immediately.

# Avocado Cucumber Salad

Serves: 4 | Prep time: 15 minutes | Cook time: n/a | Total time: 15 minutes

- 2 cucumbers, peeled and diced into large chunks
- 2½ cups halved cherry tomatoes
- 3 tablespoons minced red onion
- 2 avocados, diced
- ½ cup Feta cheese crumbles
- 1 tablespoon balsamic vinegar
- 2 tablespoons olive oil
- 1 teaspoon salt
- 1 teaspoon pepper

In a large bowl, toss together diced cucumbers, halved cherry tomatoes, and minced onion until well combined.

To bowl, add diced avocados and feta cheese. Toss gently so that the avocados and cheese do not fall apart.

In a separate bowl, whisk together vinegar, olive oil, salt, and pepper. Pour vinegar mixture over salad and toss gently until combined.

If not serving immediately, wait to add avocados to avoid them browning.

# Chicken Bowtie Salad

Serves: 10 | Prep time: 1 hour, 20 minutes | Cook time: n/a | Total time: 1 hour, 20 minutes

1 cup vegetable oil

⅔ cup teriyaki sauce

⅔ cup white wine vinegar

3 tablespoons granulated sugar

3 tablespoons brown sugar

½ teaspoon salt

½ teaspoon pepper

1 (16-ounce) package bowtie pasta, cooked al dente

2 cups cooked and chopped chicken

1 (10-ounce) bag baby spinach

3 (11-ounce) cans mandarin oranges

1 bunch green onions, thinly sliced

1 (6-ounce) bag dried cranberries

½ cup thinly sliced almonds

In a medium bowl, whisk vegetable oil, teriyaki sauce, white wine vinegar, sugars, salt, and pepper. Pour half of this marinade into a large zipper-top bag; place other half in a storage container and refrigerate until later.

Add chicken and pasta to bag with marinade in it and seal. Let pasta and chicken marinate in the fridge for at least 1 hour.

In a large bowl, mix together baby spinach, mandarin oranges, green onions, dried cranberries, and almonds. Add pasta and chicken and mix well. Add remaining marinade—as much or as little as you prefer—and mix until all ingredients are coated.

Serve and enjoy!

# TRADITIONS

## *Garden-Fresh Salsas*

Nothing beats the taste of fresh salsa in the summer! When we were growing up, our parents had a huge garden in their backyard. Even though we hated all of the weeding and watering during the summer, we always loved the results. We especially loved experimenting with new fruits and vegetables, and we loved it when our mom would make salsa. Here are a few fast and easy salsa recipes to try this year!

### Peach Salsa

2 cups chopped peaches

1 cup chopped cherry tomatoes

¼ cup chopped red onion

¼ cup chopped cilantro

1 red pepper, chopped

1 jalapeño, seeded and chopped

Juice from 1 lime

1 tablespoon honey

Combine all ingredients in a bowl and toss until evenly coated with honey and lime juice. Serve with your favorite chips and enjoy!

## Pineapple-Mango Salsa

1 mango, peeled and chopped

1 cup diced fresh pineapple

1 Roma tomato, diced

2 tablespoons chopped fresh cilantro

2 green onions, sliced

2 tablespoons lime juice

1 tablespoon lemon juice

1 jalapeño pepper, seeded and diced very small

Combine all ingredients in a bowl and toss until flavors are blended. Serve with tortilla chips or on baguettes. Best served fresh. Enjoy!

## Strawberry-Mango Salsa

1 pound strawberries, diced

1 mango, peeled and diced

½ red onion, chopped

1 jalapeño, seeded and chopped

½ tablespoon chopped cilantro

1 tablespoon honey

2 tablespoons lime juice

Combine all ingredients in a bowl and toss until flavors are blended. Serve with tortilla chips or on baguettes. Best served fresh. Enjoy!

## Pico

4 firm Roma tomatoes, diced

1 medium onion, diced

1 jalapeño pepper, diced

4 tablespoons chopped cilantro

Juice of 2 limes

1 teaspoon garlic, minced

Gently toss all ingredients in a medium bowl and refrigerate at least 2 hours for flavors to blend.

# SEPTEMBER

## *Kid-Friendly Recipes*

# Baked Broccoli Mac 'n' Cheese

Serves: 8 | Prep time: 20 minutes | Cook time: 25 minutes | Total time: 45 minutes

1   (12-ounce) package elbow macaroni

2   cups broccoli florets

1½  tablespoons butter

¼   cup minced onion

¼   cup all-purpose flour

2   cups milk

1   cup fat-free chicken broth

Salt and pepper, to taste

2   cups shredded cheddar cheese

¼   cup Italian seasoned breadcrumbs

2   tablespoons butter, melted

Preheat oven to 375 degrees F. Spray a 9x13-inch baking dish with nonstick cooking spray.

Bring a large pot of salted water to a boil, add pasta and broccoli, and cook according to package directions for al dente. Drain and set aside while preparing sauce.

In a large saucepan over medium heat, melt 1½ tablespoons butter.

Add onion and cook over low heat about 2 minutes.

Add flour and cook another minute, or until the flour is golden brown and the mixture is well combined.

Increase temperature to medium-high and whisk in milk and chicken broth. Cook, stirring often, for 5 minutes, or until sauce begins to bubble and becomes smooth and thick. Season with salt and pepper to taste.

Once the sauce is thick, remove from heat, add cheese, and mix well until cheese is melted.

Add cooked macaroni and broccoli and mix well.

Pour into prepared baking dish.

In a small bowl, combine seasoned breadcrumbs and 2 tablespoons melted butter. Sprinkle over top of pasta.

Bake 20 to 25 minutes, or until top is golden brown.

# Oatmeal Crème Pies

Serves: 24 | Prep time: 20 minutes | Cook time: 10 minutes | Total time: 30 minutes

¾ cup butter, softened

1 cup brown sugar

½ cup granulated sugar

2 eggs

1½ teaspoons vanilla extract

1 tablespoon molasses

2 cups all-purpose flour

¼ teaspoon baking soda

1 teaspoon baking powder

¼ teaspoon salt

1¼ teaspoons ground cinnamon

¼ teaspoon ground cloves

¼ teaspoon ground nutmeg

2 cups rolled oats

1 recipe Crème Pie Frosting

Preheat oven to 375 degrees F. Line baking sheets with parchment paper.

In a large bowl with an electric mixer, cream together butter, brown sugar, and sugar on medium speed until light and creamy, about 2 minutes.

Add eggs, vanilla, and molasses and mix until well combined.

In a medium bowl whisk together the flour, baking soda, baking powder, salt, cinnamon, cloves, nutmeg, and oats.

Slowly add the dry ingredients to the wet ingredients. The dough will be thick and may need to be mixed by hand at the end.

Roll dough into 1-inch balls and place on prepared baking sheets. Cook 10 minutes, until cookies are golden around the edge.

Cool on cookie sheet 2 minutes before transferring to a wire rack to cool completely.

While the cookies are cooling, prepare the Crème Pie Frosting. Spread 1 to 2 tablespoons Crème Pie Frosting on the flat side of a cookie and top with another cookie, flat side down. Repeat to fill remaining cookies.

## Crème Pie Frosting

½ cup butter, softened

2½ to 3 cups powdered sugar

2 tablespoons heavy cream

1 teaspoon vanilla

Pinch salt

In a medium bowl, with an electric mixer, beat butter for about 1 minute, until creamy. Add powdered sugar, heavy cream, vanilla, and salt. Beat on high until smooth and creamy, about 3 minutes.

# Rice Krispies Apples

Serves: 10 | Prep time: 10 minutes | Cook time: 10 minutes | Total time: 20 minutes

| | |
|---|---|
| 6 cups Rice Krispies cereal | 1½ teaspoons red food coloring |
| ¼ cup butter, divided | Pretzel rods |
| 4 cups mini-marshmallows | Green Laffy Taffy for apple leaves |

Melt butter in a medium saucepan over medium heat. Once fully melted and foaming, add the mini-marshmallows and mix until smooth and completely melted. Add the food coloring and stir until color is evenly distributed.

Remove from heat and stir in the Rice Krispies, mixing well until all cereal is coated.

Butter your hands or spray with nonstick cooking spray and form mixture into apple shapes about 4 inches in diameter. Rest apples on parchment or waxed paper.

Stick a pretzel rod in the top middle of each "apple" and cut a piece of Laffy Taffy into a leaf shape and place next to the "stem."

# Baked Cheeseburger Sliders

Serves: 6 | Prep time: 10 minutes | Cook time: 30 minutes | Total time: 40 minutes

2 pounds lean ground beef

½ onion, diced

¼ cup bread crumbs

½ cup barbecue sauce

½ teaspoon seasoned salt

Freshly ground black pepper to taste

6 slices cheddar cheese

12 small slider rolls, such as King's Hawaiian

Heat oven to 400 degrees F.

In a large bowl, combine beef, onion, bread crumbs, barbecue sauce, salt, and pepper. Gently press mixture into a 9x13-inch baking pan so that it makes one large patty of even thickness. Use the tines of a fork to poke holes throughout the meat. Bake 30 minutes.

When the hamburger is fully cooked, the meat will shrink away from the sides and liquid will accumulate around the edges of pan. At this point, remove the pan from oven and carefully drain off the liquid.

Place slices of cheese in a single layer on top of the meat and return pan to oven 2 to 3 minutes, or until the cheese starts to melt. Remove from the oven and allow to rest for a few minutes. Cut the meat into 2-inch squares, making 12 mini-hamburgers. Serve with dill pickle slices, ketchup, mustard, tomatoes, and lettuce.

# Mini Corn Dog Muffins

Serves: 6 to 8 | Prep time: 10 minutes | Cook time: 12 minutes | Total time: 22 minutes

½ cup butter, melted

½ cup granulated sugar

2 eggs

1 cup buttermilk

½ teaspoon baking soda

1 cup cornmeal

1 cup all-purpose flour

½ teaspoon salt

8 to 10 all-beef hot dogs, cut into 1-inch pieces

Preheat oven to 375 degrees F.

Combine butter and sugar in a large bowl and whisk to combine.

Add eggs and buttermilk and whisk until well combined.

In a separate bowl, combine baking soda, cornmeal, flour, and salt. Stir to combine.

Whisk dry ingredients into wet ingredients and stir until combined.

Spray a mini muffin tin with nonstick cooking spray, and spoon 1 tablespoon of batter into each mini muffin cup.

Place one piece of hot dog into the middle of each cup.

Bake 8 to 12 minutes, or until cornbread is golden brown.

Cool in mini muffin tin 5 minutes before serving.

# Parmesan Sesame Chicken Strips with Honey-Mustard Dipping Sauce

Serves: 4 to 5 | Prep time: 15 minutes | Cook time: 18 minutes | Total time: 33 minutes

| | |
|---|---|
| 4 boneless, skinless chicken breasts | 1 cup light mayonnaise |
| 35 Ritz crackers | 2 teaspoons dried minced onion |
| ¼ cup sesame seeds | 2 teaspoons ground mustard |
| ¼ cup grated Parmesan cheese | |

Preheat oven to 425 degrees F. Line a large baking sheet with aluminum foil and lightly spray foil with nonstick cooking spray.

Cut chicken lengthwise into ¼-inch strips and set aside.

Place crackers in a large, zipper-top bag, seal, and roll over crackers with a rolling pin until they are finely crushed.

In a shallow bowl, combine crushed crackers, sesame seeds, and Parmesan cheese. In a second shallow bowl, combine mayonnaise, onion, and mustard. Dip chicken strips into mayonnaise mixture, then into crumb mixture. Place chicken on prepared baking sheet.

Bake 15 to 18 minutes. Serve with Honey-Mustard Dipping Sauce.

## Honey-Mustard Dipping Sauce

| | |
|---|---|
| ½ cup mayonnaise | 3 tablespoons honey |
| 2 tablespoons yellow mustard | ½ tablespoon lemon juice |
| 1 tablespoon Dijon mustard | |

Combine all ingredients and enjoy!

# Quick-and-Easy Calzones

Serves: 6 | Prep time: 10 minutes | Cook time: 10 minutes | Total time: 20 minutes

1 (13.8-ounce) can refrigerated pizza crust

½ cup pizza sauce

1 cup shredded mozzarella cheese

18 slices pepperoni

1 tablespoon butter, melted

Italian seasoning, to taste

Grated Parmesan cheese, to taste

Preheat oven to 400 degrees F. Spray baking sheet with nonstick cooking spray.

Roll out the pizza crust and cut it into 6 equal-sized squares.

In the middle of each square, place a portion of the pizza sauce, shredded cheese, and pepperoni.

Fold the dough over into a triangle and use a fork to press along the edges of the triangle to seal it.

Place calzones on the prepared baking sheet. Brush the top of each calzone with butter, then sprinkle with Italian seasoning and grated Parmesan cheese.

Place in the oven and bake 10 to 12 minutes, or until tops are golden brown. Serve warm with extra pizza sauce for dipping.

# Malibu Chicken Crescents

Serves: 16 | Prep time: 10 minutes | Cook time: 15 minutes | Total time: 25 minutes

2  (8-ounce) cans refrigerated crescent rolls

16  slices Swiss cheese

16  small slices deli ham

16  chicken strips, such as Tyson Grilled & Ready Chicken Breast Strips

2  tablespoons mustard

3  tablespoons mayonnaise

1  teaspoon Worcestershire sauce

½  teaspoon garlic powder

1  teaspoon honey

Preheat oven to 350 degrees F.

Separate dough into 16 equal pieces.

Place one slice of cheese, folded in half, one slice of ham, and one chicken strip on the larger end of a dough triangle.

Roll the crescent up with the chicken, ham, and cheese inside, and place it tip side down on a baking sheet.

Bake 15 minutes, or until tops are golden brown.

While triangles bake, prepare sauce by combining mustard, mayonnaise, Worcestershire sauce, garlic powder, and honey in a small bowl.

Serve triangles warm with sauce on the side.

# Slow Cooker Ranch Chicken Enchiladas

Serves: 8 | Prep time: 20 minutes | Cook time: 4 hours, 30 minutes | Total time: 4 hours, 50 minutes

4   boneless, skinless chicken breasts

1   (1.25-ounce) package taco seasoning

1   (1-ounce) package dry ranch dressing mix

1   (15-ounce) can chicken broth

½   cup bottled ranch dressing, plus more for topping

½   cup salsa

2   cups shredded cheddar cheese

8 to 10   flour tortillas

Cilantro (optional)

Spray slow cooker with nonstick cooking spray and place chicken inside.

Sprinkle taco seasoning and ranch dressing mix over chicken.

Pour chicken broth over chicken in slow cooker and cook on low 3 to 4 hours.

Remove chicken from slow cooker and shred with two forks.

In a small bowl, mix together ranch dressing and salsa; set aside.

Preheat oven to 350 degrees F. Spray a 9x13-inch baking pan with nonstick cooking spray and spread a thin layer of salsa/ranch mixture on the bottom of the pan.

Assemble enchiladas by spreading a few spoonsful of the salsa/ranch mixture on each tortilla. Add shredded chicken and cheese on top and roll up.

Place enchiladas seam-side down in the prepared pan and sprinkle any remaining cheese on top. Bake 30 minutes, until cheese is bubbly and nicely browned.

Drizzle with ranch dressing and sprinkle chopped cilantro on top before serving, if desired.

# Chicken Club Quesadillas

Serves: 8 | Prep time: 10 minutes | Cook time: 15 minutes | Total time: 25 minutes

- 8 flour tortillas
- 8 slices deli-sliced chicken breast
- 8 slices deli-sliced ham
- 8 slices cheddar cheese

- 8 strips bacon, cooked crisp

  Favorite sandwich toppings, such as mayonnaise, mustard, tomato, lettuce, pickles, banana peppers, etc.

  Olive oil

If using a sauce, such as mayonnaise or mustard, spread on each of the tortillas. If not using a sauce, skip this step. Layer the chicken, ham, cheese, bacon, and other toppings on half of each tortilla, fold the tortilla over and press down when you are finished putting toppings on it.

Heat a skillet over medium heat. Lightly brush olive oil on both sides of the tortilla. Cook two filled tortillas at a time, 3 to 4 minutes each, until they are golden brown, turning over once.

# TRADITIONS

## *Healthy After-School Snacks*

Never know what to feed your kids when they get home from school (or how to beat that three o'clock hunger attack)? We have fifteen great ideas—from low-calorie snacks like dill pickles to sweet berry smoothies that hide a full serving of spinach—so you can feel good about feeding your kids these quick-and-easy after-school snacks!

### Olive + Cheese + Pickle Kebabs

Cut a cheese stick into 5 (½-inch) pieces. Cut 5 sweet pickles in half. For each kebab, thread 1 olive, 1 pickle piece, and 1 piece of cheese on a toothpick. Makes 5 mini-kebabs.

### Cucumber Boats

Take 1 cucumber, peel it (if desired), slice it in half, and scoop out the seeds. Fill each half with about a ½ cup low-fat cottage cheese. Top with salt and pepper to taste. Serves 2.

### Green Berry Smoothie

Add ½ cup apple juice, 1 cup spinach, 1 banana, and 1 cup frozen mixed berries in a blender and blend until smooth. Add water to reach desired consistency. Serves 2.

## Hummus and Veggies

Serve hummus with your favorite sliced vegetables. We love peppers, sugar snap peas, carrots, and celery.

## Ants on a Log

Wash 5 celery stalks and cut them in half. Spread the inside of each celery piece with 1 to 2 tablespoons of your favorite nut butter (we love peanut butter and almond butter). Top with raisins and serve. Serves 5.

## Monkey Tails

- 5 large bananas, peeled and sliced in two halves
- 2 cups chocolate chips
- 2 teaspoons vegetable oil

  Toppings, such as chopped peanuts, almonds, coconut, or granola
- 10 (6-inch) skewers

Insert a skewer into the cut end of a halved banana. Place each banana on a baking sheet covered with waxed paper. Freeze 1 to 2 hours, or until bananas are frozen.

In a microwave-safe bowl, mix together chocolate chips and vegetable oil. Microwave on high power for 30 seconds, then remove and stir. Continue heating and stirring in 30-second intervals until the chocolate is completely smooth.

Remove bananas from the freezer. One at a time, dip each banana in the chocolate mixture and sprinkle with your favorite toppings, holding it above a plate and rotating it slowly so there are toppings covering the entire banana. Place each banana back on the waxed paper and return to the freezer until the chocolate is firm, about 30 minutes. Serves 10.

### Peanut Butter Yogurt Dip

Mix together ½ cup strawberry yogurt, ½ cup peanut butter, and ¼ cup powdered sugar until it is smooth and creamy. Serve with your favorite fruits. Serves 4.

### Turkey Roll-Ups

Place a piece of turkey on a piece of lettuce. Spread a dollop of mustard on the turkey slice. Place a pickle spear (cut in half lengthwise) in the middle of the turkey slice. Roll it up and secure it with a toothpick.

### Frozen Yogurt-Covered Raspberries

Wash 1 to 2 cups raspberries and let them dry completely. Place a sheet of waxed paper on a cookie sheet that will fit in your freezer. Use a toothpick to dip raspberries into Greek yogurt. Place on waxed paper, and transport to freezer using cutting board to help with the transfer. Freeze completely and serve cold.

### Mini Cucumber Sandwiches

Slice a cucumber into ¼-inch thick rounds. Between two cucumber rounds, stack cheese, tomatoes, and deli meat (and anything else you like on your sandwiches). Serve cold. Serves 4 to 6.

### Yogurt Parfaits

Spoon ½ cup yogurt into four separate small bowls. Top each bowl with ¼ cup granola, and a handful of berries.

### Pita Nachos

Split 2 whole-wheat (6-inch) tortillas into 6 tri-angles each. Brush with olive oil and bake at 350 degrees F. on a cookie sheet for 5 minutes, or until crispy. Re-move from oven and top each with a pinch of shredded mozzarella cheese and a small spoon-ful of pico de gallo. Bake an additional 10 to 12 minutes, until cheese has melted. Serves 6 to 8.

### Chicken Pinwheels

Cover a tortilla with a wedge of spreadable cheese. Layer sliced chicken breast, lettuce, cucumber slices, and tomatoes atop the cheese. Roll up and cut into slices. Serves 2.

### Banana Chips

Slice 4 to 5 bananas into 1/8-inch thick slices and place on a foil-lined baking sheet. Brush with lemon juice and bake at 200 degrees F. for 1 hour. Remove from the oven and flip, then return to the oven and bake for an-other hour, or until crispy. Remove from the oven and let them cool. The longer they cool, the more firm they will become.

### Chocolate Trail Mix

In a large bowl, mix together 2 cups of walnuts, 2 cups of mini pretzels, 1 cup raisins, 1 cup golden raisins, and 1 cup dark choco-late pieces. Serves 6 to 8.

# OCTOBER

*Treats for a Spooky Halloween Party*

# Mummy Donut Holes

Serves: 24 | Prep time: 20 minutes | Cook time: n/a | Total time: 20 minutes

1  (1-pound) package white chocolate candy coating or almond bark, divided

24  donut holes

Black gel frosting

Melt ¾ of the white chocolate candy coating in a bowl according to package directions.

Dip each donut hole in the chocolate, making sure to cover entire donut hole with chocolate. Remove from chocolate using two forks, letting excess chocolate drip back into the bowl.

Place donut hole on baking sheet covered with parchment paper and let sit for 30 minutes to an hour so that the chocolate can harden (if desired, you can put them in the fridge and they will set up faster).

Melt remaining white chocolate and, using a spoon, drizzle "mummy lines" on each donut hole, leaving a little room for the eyes. Let harden for about 30 minutes.

Place two black gel dots on each donut hole for eyes and serve.

# Candy Corn Cupcakes

Serves: 24 | Prep time: 15 minutes | Cook time: 20 minutes | Total time: 35 minutes

1 (15.25-ounce) white cake mix

Ingredients called for on cake mix (oil, eggs, water)

Yellow and red food coloring

Buttercream Frosting (see recipe on page 25 or use your favorite recipe)

Candy corn for garnish (optional)

Preheat oven to 350 degrees F. Line muffin tins with 24 cupcake liners.

Prepare cake batter as directed on package. Divide batter equally into three small bowls. Leave the first bowl of batter white. In the second bowl, add about 12 drops yellow food coloring. Stir well; add more coloring if you'd like a brighter yellow. In the third bowl, add 15 drops yellow food coloring and 5 drops red food coloring to make an orange batter.

In each cupcake liner, drop a spoonful or 2 of yellow batter and spread the batter to the edges of the liner as evenly as possible. When yellow batter is all gone, repeat the process with the orange batter, making sure to spread the orange all the way to the edges so no yellow batter is showing. Finally, repeat with the white batter, once again spreading it to the edges so no orange batter shows.

Bake cupcakes according to directions on package. When they are finished cooking, remove from oven and let cool.

Pipe frosting onto cupcakes and top with a candy corn for garnish.

# Homemade Root Beer

Serves: 40 | Prep time: 15 minutes | Brewing time: 45 | Total time: 60 minutes

6  cups granulated sugar

4  gallons water

1  (2-ounce) bottle root beer extract

5  pounds dry ice

In a large container or cooler, mix together sugar and water until all sugar is dissolved. Stir in root beer extract. Carefully add dry ice to cooler. If needed, use ice pick to break ice apart. Let mixture brew for at least 45 minutes before serving.

# Mini Donut Scary Eyes

Serves: 12 | Prep time: 5 minutes | Cook time: n/a | Total time: 5 minutes

Small powdered donuts

Gummy Lifesavers

Chocolate chips

1   tube red frosting or red gel

Use the red frosting gel to draw 5 or 6 lines from the center of the donut to the outer edges to resemble bloodshot eyes. Place the lifesaver over the hole in the center of the donut. Push down gently so the lifesaver can stick to the donut with the frosting holding it all together. Put a little frosting on the bottom of a chocolate chip and put it on top of the Lifesaver, using frosting gel as glue.

# White Chocolate Monster Munch

Serves: 12 | Prep time: 15 minutes | Cook time: 3 minutes | Total time: 18 minutes

½ (10-ounce) package mini pretzel twists

2½ cups Honey Nut Cheerios

2½ cups Corn Chex cereal

1 cup peanuts (or mixed nuts)

1 (12-ounce) package candy corn M&M's

2 cups candy corn

1 (12-ounce) package white chocolate chips

1½ tablespoons vegetable oil

In a very large bowl (or two medium bowls), combine the first 6 ingredients. Set aside.

In a microwave-safe bowl, melt white chocolate chips and vegetable oil on high power in 30-second intervals, stirring between each interval, until chocolate is smooth and melted.

Pour melted chocolate over cereal mixture and stir until all the cereal is evenly covered with white chocolate. Spread mixture on 2 large baking sheets lined with waxed paper. Let cool and then break apart into chunks.

Store in an airtight container.

# Melted Witch Cupcakes

Serves: 24 | Prep time: 35 minutes | Cook time: 22 minutes | Total time: 57 minutes

3 eggs

½ cup oil

¾ cup milk

½ cup sour cream

3 teaspoons vanilla extract, divided

1 (15.25-ounce) chocolate cake mix

1 cup chocolate chips

2 cups butter, softened

2½ cups powdered sugar

2 (7-ounce) jars marshmallow crème

8 ounces white baking chocolate

½ cup heavy cream

Green food coloring

12 striped paper straws, cut in half

Witch boots (black cardstock, cut into the shape of a boot)

To make cupcakes: Preheat oven to 350 degrees F. and line muffin tins with cupcake liners.

In a large bowl, add the eggs, oil, milk, sour cream, and 2 teaspoons vanilla extract and mix until thoroughly combined. Add in the cake mix and stir until smooth. Fold in chocolate chips.

Fill cupcake liners about ¾ of the way full, then bake for 18 to 22 minutes until a toothpick inserted in center comes out clean.

To make frosting: In a large bowl with an electric mixer, beat the butter on medium-high speed for 4 to 5 minutes, stopping to scrape the bowl once or twice.

Reduce the speed to low and slowly add the powdered sugar. You can add more or less powdered sugar depending on how thick you want your icing.

Once the powdered sugar is all incorporated, add in vanilla extract and marshmallow crème, mixing well until thick and smooth. Pipe frosting onto each cupcake.

To make ganache: Break the white chocolate into small pieces and place in a heat-resistant bowl. In a small saucepan, heat the heavy cream until just boiling, then remove from heat and pour over white chocolate. Mix thoroughly until white chocolate is completely melted.

Add green food coloring, 1 to 2 drops at a time, until the white chocolate reaches the desired shade of green. Drizzle ganache over frosting.

Glue witch boots to the straw halves, and stick two legs into each cupcake with the boots facing out.

# Candy Corn Fudge

Yields: 24 pieces | Prep time: 3 hours | Cook time: n/a | Total time: 3 hours

| | |
|---|---|
| 4 cups white chocolate chips, divided | Yellow food coloring |
| 2 (12-ounce) tubs vanilla frosting | Red food coloring |

Line an 8x8-inch pan with waxed paper that has been sprayed with nonstick cooking spray.

Place 1⅓ cups white chocolate chips in a microwave-safe bowl and melt on high power in 30-second intervals, stirring between each interval, until chips are completely smooth.

Add approximately ⅓ of the frosting to the melted chocolate, along with a few drops of yellow food coloring.

Stir to combine and adjust the shade to your desired color.

Pour the yellow fudge into the prepared pan and refrigerate until mostly set, about 20 minutes. The fudge does not have to be rock hard but should be set enough so that it doesn't move when the pan is tilted.

Place 1⅓ cups white chocolate chips in a microwave-safe bowl and melt on high power in 30-second intervals, stirring between each interval, until chips are completely smooth.

Add approximately ⅓ of the frosting to the melted chocolate, along with a few drops of yellow food coloring and a few drops of red food coloring

Stir to combine and adjust the shade of orange to your desired color.

Pour the orange-colored fudge over the yellow fudge, smooth it in an even layer, and return to the refrigerator to allow the new layer to set, about 20 minutes.

Place remaining white chocolate chips in a microwave-safe bowl and melt on high power in 30-second intervals, stirring between each interval, until chips are completely smooth.

Add remaining ⅓ of the frosting to the melted chocolate and stir well to combine.

Pour the white fudge over the orange layer and return to the refrigerator once more and allow it to set fully, about 2 hours.

To serve, cut the fudge into 1-inch squares. Be sure to use a large knife with a smooth blade and wipe the blade frequently to ensure that the sides of the fudge squares do not get smeared with other colors. Store fudge in an airtight container in the refrigerator.

# Spooky Smile Cookies

Yields: 24 cookies | Prep time: 10 minutes | Cook time: 12 minutes | Total time: 22 minutes

1 cup butter, at room temperature

1 cup brown sugar

1 cup granulated sugar

1½ cups peanut butter

2 eggs

3 cups all-purpose flour

1 teaspoon baking soda

1 teaspoon vanilla extract

Additional sugar, for rolling cookie dough

1 cup Nutella

1 (10-ounce) bag mini-marshmallows

Preheat oven to 350 degrees F.

In a large bowl, cream together butter, sugars, and peanut butter with an electric mixer. Add eggs, flour, baking soda, and vanilla extract and mix well.

Roll dough into 1-inch balls, roll in sugar, place on an ungreased cookie sheet, and use a fork to make a crisscross design on top. Bake 10 to 12 minutes, or until golden brown.

Let cookies cool completely. Spread Nutella on the smooth side of each cookie. Cut the cookies in half horizontally. Line the rounded edge of one cookie half with marshmallows and place another cookie half on top to make a smile!

# Gingerbread Mummy Cookies

Serves: 30 | Prep time: 15 minutes | Cook time: 8 minutes | Total time: 23 minutes

¾ cup margarine, softened

1 cup granulated sugar

¼ teaspoon salt

1 egg

¼ cup molasses

1 teaspoon cinnamon

½ teaspoon ground cloves

1 teaspoon ground ginger

1¼ teaspoons baking soda

3 cups all-purpose flour

4 tablespoons butter, softened

4 ounces cream cheese, softened

½ teaspoon vanilla extract

1 teaspoon milk

3 cups powdered sugar

60 candy eyeballs

To make cookies: In a large bowl with an electric mixer, cream together margarine, sugar, salt, egg, and molasses. Add cinnamon, cloves, ginger, baking soda, and flour and mix well.

Chill in refrigerator 30 minutes.

Preheat oven to 350 degrees F. Roll out dough on a floured surface to about ¼-inch thick. Use a gingerbread-man-shaped cookie cutter to cut cookies.

Place cut cookies on an ungreased baking sheet and bake 8 to 9 minutes. Cool for a few minutes on cookie sheet before removing to a wire rack to cool completely.

To make frosting: In a large bowl, mix together butter, cream cheese, vanilla, and 1 teaspoon milk with a hand mixer. Gradually add in powdered sugar.

If too runny, add more powdered sugar; if too thick, add a little more milk.

Pipe icing onto cooled cookies to look like mummy wraps. Stick on candy eyeballs with a little dot of frosting on the back of each eyeball.

# Dinner in a Pumpkin

Serves: 6 | Prep time: 25 minutes | Cook time: 1 hour, 15 minutes | Total time: 1 hour, 40 minutes

1  medium pumpkin (see note)

1  tablespoon olive oil

2  cups chopped assorted vegetables, such as celery, carrots, onions, green pepper, sweet potatoes, mushrooms, etc.

1  pound lean ground turkey

1  tablespoon soy sauce

1  (14.5-ounce) can condensed cream of chicken soup

2  cups prepared brown rice

Cut off the top of the pumpkin and thoroughly clean out pulp and seeds.

Preheat oven to 350 degrees F.

Heat oil in a large skillet over medium heat, add assorted veggies, and sauté until tender. Add meat, breaking up into small pieces and cooking until browned.

Stir in soy sauce, soup, and cooked brown rice. Mix well.

Spoon mixture into cleaned pumpkin shell. Replace pumpkin top and place entire pumpkin on a baking sheet.

Bake 1 hour, or until inside meat of the pumpkin is tender.

After you scoop out the yummy stuff inside, don't forget to scrape out the insides of the pumpkin! It tastes just like spaghetti squash!

*Note:* Check the size of your oven to make sure the pumpkin will fit.

# TRADITIONS

## *Halloween Party Activities*

Our family Halloween party has always been one of the biggest events of the year. One year, we even had a spook alley, set up by Grandpa Tom. As soon as we got to the end of the spook alley, we would run back to the entrance so we could go through it again. Our love of Halloween runs deep. We go all out with carnival games, prizes, getting spooked, and, of course, tons of great food!

Here are a few of the fun games we play that involve kids of all ages.

1. **Monster Munch:** Make a monster from a large piece of cardboard, ensuring that the mouth is large enough for a child to stick his arm through. Set up the monster on a card table and have the kids reach through the mouth to pull out a prize. Hide the prize in a huge pot of cold, cooked spaghetti noodles they have to dig through to find.

2. **Dead Hand Ring Toss:** Cover a large piece of cardboard with orange butcher paper and splatter it with red paint. Glue skeleton hands (purchased at a dollar store) all over the cardboard. Give the kids glow necklaces to serve as the rings for the Dead Hand Ring Toss.

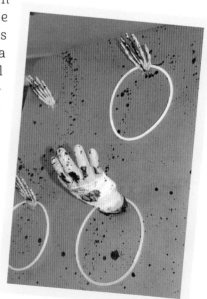

3. **Spooky Can Knock Down:** Use acrylic paint to decorate a bunch of old soup and vegetable cans. If you want, put faces on the cans to resemble ghosts, jack-o-lanterns, monsters, and so on. Stack the cans in a pyramid and let the kids use a tennis ball to knock them over. You could make 2 sets of cans and hold a relay where each person on a team must knock down all the cans in the pyramid, put the pyramid back up, then run and pass the tennis ball to the next person in line. The team that goes through its whole line first wins!

4. **Pin the Bowtie on Mr. Skeleton:** Draw or trace a skeleton on a large sheet of white butcher paper. Have the kids stand in a line and take turns trying to stick a paper bowtie on Mr. Skeleton after being blindfolded and spun around a few times.

5. **Indoor Trick-or-Treating:** Hang a pumpkin on all the doorknobs in the house. Fill each pumpkin with treats the kids can grab as they go from room to room. Play spooky music, dim the lights, and decorate each room with hanging spiders or other scary items the kids will encounter as they search for treats. If you want, have someone hiding in a room or two to scare the indoor trick-or-treaters or make it seem like a ghost is talking whenever a child picks a piece of candy.

6. **Donut on a String:** String a long piece of yarn from one wall to another so it spans the room. Then tie shorter strings around donuts and attach these strings to the longer string so you have a line of donuts hanging down at mouth level for most kids. The kids then have to eat a donut without using their hands.

7. **Mummy Wrap:** Divide the party into groups of 3 or 4 people each. One person from each group will be the mummy. Each team is given a roll of toilet-paper. Everyone starts at the same time and wraps their mummy as fast as they can. The first group to get to the center of the toilet-paper roll is the winner.

9. **Creepy Feel Bowl Game:** For this game, have 7 bowls set out on a table. Fill each bowl with the following:

- peeled grapes for zombie eyeballs
- spaghetti noodles for rat intestines
- raisins for witches' warts
- peeled tomatoes for hearts
- cooked rice mixed with some oil or water for maggots
- corn husk silk for vampire hair
- mini-marshmallows mixed with a little oil for Frankenstein's monster's brain

Blindfold a child and then guide them to the table and let them feel each bowl. Tell them what things they could possibly be feeling and then guess which is which.

8. **Halloween Version of Don't Eat Pete:** Divide an orange poster board into 9 squares. In each square, tape a picture of something that relates to Halloween, such as a candy corn, a Frankenstein face, a spider, and so on. Place the poster on a table and then put a mini M&M's candy on each square.

Have one person leave the room while the rest of the group chooses which square will be Pete. Call the person back into the room, where he or she will slowly start picking M&M's to eat. Have everyone be completely silent as the person chooses which M&M's to eat.

As soon as the person grabs the M&M's candy from the square designated as "Pete," everyone yells, "Trick or treat—don't eat Pete!" as loud as they can. It's hilarious to watch how startled the person is. Kids start laughing hysterically and love taking turns getting scared.

# NOVEMBER

*Recipes for a Thanksgiving Feast*

# Creamy Green Bean Casserole

Serves: 12 | Prep time: 20 minutes | Cook time: 30 minutes | Total time: 50 minutes

1 (6-ounce) package chicken stuffing mix

1 tablespoon butter

1 pound fresh green beans, trimmed and cut into 1-inch lengths

½ teaspoon black pepper

¼ cup all-purpose flour

1¾ cups chicken broth

1 (8-ounce) brick cream cheese, cubed

Prepare stuffing according to package directions.

In a large skillet over medium heat, melt butter and then stir in the beans. Let them cook for about 6 minutes, or until beans are crisp-tender. Sprinkle with flour and pepper and stir for an additional minute. Stir in broth and let simmer for 3 minutes, stirring frequently. Add cream cheese and stir until melted.

Spray a 9x13-inch pan with nonstick cooking spray.

Spoon beans into the prepared pan. Sprinkle stuffing on top, cover, and refrigerate up to 24 hours before baking.

Cook, uncovered, at 400 degrees F. for 30 minutes, or until heated through.

# Make-Ahead Mashed Potatoes

Serves: 10 | Prep time: 25 minutes | Cook time: 30 minutes | Total time: 55 minutes

3 to 3½ pounds Yukon Gold potatoes, cubed (see note)

2 tablespoons butter

4 ounces cream cheese, softened

⅔ cup sour cream

¼ cup whole milk or heavy cream

¾ teaspoon salt

Additional butter (optional)

Fresh parsley (optional)

Paprika (optional)

Place potatoes in a large stockpot and add enough water to cover potatoes. Bring water to a boil, cover with lid. Reduce heat to medium and cook 20 to 25 minutes, or until potatoes are fork-tender. Drain off water.

Transfer the potatoes to a large bowl and mash with a potato masher.

Mix in butter, cream cheese, sour cream, milk, and salt until completely combined.

Spray a 9x13-inch baking pan with nonstick cooking spray. Scoop mashed potatoes into the prepared pan.

If desired, brush the top of the potatoes with additional melted butter, fresh parsley, and paprika.

If you are making these potatoes for later, cover the potatoes and refrigerate up to 24 hours in advance. When you are ready to bake them, let the potatoes sit at room temperature for about 30 minutes before putting them in the oven.

Preheat oven to 350 degrees F. and bake uncovered 25 to 30 minutes, or until the potatoes are heated all the way through.

*Note:* If desired, you can peel the potatoes, but we love the ease of leaving the potatoes unpeeled.

# Homemade Creamed Corn

Serves: 6 to 8 | Prep time: 5 minutes | Cook time: 15 minutes | Total time: 20 minutes

2   (20-ounce) packages frozen corn kernels

1   cup heavy cream

1   cup milk

1   teaspoon salt

2   teaspoons granulated sugar

⅛   teaspoon white pepper

2   tablespoons butter, melted

2   tablespoons all-purpose flour

Combine frozen corn kernels, cream, milk, salt, sugar, and white pepper in a large pot and bring to a boil over medium-high heat. Meanwhile, whisk together melted butter and flour in a separate bowl and then stir into boiling corn mixture. Continue to cook, stirring constantly, until mixture is thickened, about 1 to 2 minutes.

# Mom's Sweet Potato Casserole

Serves: 12 | Prep time: 20 minutes | Cook time: 25 minutes | Total time: 45 minutes

- 2 pounds sweet potatoes, peeled and chopped
- ½ cup granulated sugar
- ¼ cup evaporated milk
- 5 tablespoons butter, melted and divided
- ½ plus ⅛ teaspoons salt
- 1 teaspoon vanilla extract
- 2 large eggs
- ⅓ cup all-purpose flour
- ⅔ cup packed brown sugar
- ½ cup chopped pecans

Preheat oven to 350 degrees F. Spray a 9x13-inch, broiler-safe baking dish with nonstick cooking spray.

Place a pot of water on the stove and bring the water to a boil. Add peeled and chopped potatoes and cook 10 to 15 minutes, or until the potatoes are tender.

Remove potatoes to a large bowl; add granulated sugar, milk, 3 tablespoons of the melted butter, ½ teaspoon salt, and vanilla. Beat with an electric mixer at medium speed until smooth. Add eggs and beat well. Pour potato mixture into prepared pan and set aside while preparing topping.

To prepare topping: whisk together flour, brown sugar, and ⅛ teaspoon salt. Stir in remaining 2 tablespoons melted butter. Sprinkle flour mixture evenly over potato mixture; arrange pecans evenly over top. Bake 25 minutes or just until golden brown.

Remove casserole from oven. Preheat broiler and then return casserole to oven and broil 45 seconds, or until topping is bubbly. Let stand 5 minutes before serving.

# Butternut Squash Bake

Serves: 6 | Prep time: 10 minutes | Cook time: 50 minutes | Total time: 1 hour

- 1 butternut squash
- ¼ cup butter, melted
- 2 cloves garlic, chopped
- ½ cup Italian seasoned bread crumbs
- ½ cup grated Parmesan cheese
- Salt and pepper to taste

Preheat oven to 375 degrees F. Grease a 9x13-inch pan and set aside.

Wash and peel squash. Slice squash vertically down the center and remove seeds. Slice squash halves into ½-inch slices. Arrange slices in rows in pan.

In a small bowl, combine butter, garlic, breadcrumbs, and Parmesan cheese. Sprinkle mixture over squash, making sure each slice is coated with cheese and breadcrumbs. Sprinkle with salt and pepper.

Bake 45 to 50 minutes, or until squash is cooked all the way through and topping begins to turn golden brown.

# Zucchini Parmesan Bake

Serves: 8 | Prep time: 15 minutes | Cook time: 15 minutes | Total time: 30 minutes

| | |
|---|---|
| 3 tablespoons olive oil | 1 cup frozen corn |
| ½ cup chopped red onions | ½ cup shredded mozzarella cheese |
| 1 clove garlic, crushed | ¼ cup grated Parmesan |
| 4 medium zucchini, chopped | Salt and pepper to taste |

Preheat oven to 350 degrees F.

In large skillet, heat olive oil over medium high heat, add onions and garlic, and cook and stir 5 minutes, or until onions are tender. Stir in zucchini; cook 8 to 10 minutes, or until zucchini is lightly browned, stirring occasionally. Remove from heat and add corn, cheeses, and salt and pepper to taste.

Place in a 9x9-inch pan and bake, uncovered, 15 minutes. Remove and serve.

# Golden Sweet Cornbread

Serves: 6 to 8 | Prep time: 5 minutes | Cook time: 15 minutes | Total time: 20 minutes

| | |
|---|---|
| 1 (15.25-ounce) yellow cake mix | 1 cup water |
| 2 (8.5-ounce) corn muffin mixes | ⅓ cup oil |
| 5 eggs | ½ cup milk |

Preheat oven to 350 degrees F. Spray a 9x13-inch baking pan with nonstick cooking spray and set aside.

In a large bowl, whisk together dry cake mix and both corn muffin mixes. Add eggs, water, oil, and milk.

Stir well to combine ingredients, but do not overmix. Pour batter into prepared pan and bake 25 to 30 minutes, or until a toothpick inserted in the center comes out clean.

Serve warm with butter and honey.

# Thanksgiving Turkey

Serves: 10 to 12 | Prep time: 15 minutes | Cook time: 3 hours+ | Total time: 3 hours, 15 minutes

- 1 (10- to 12-pound) whole turkey (see note)
- 1 cup butter, softened
- 2 teaspoons minced garlic
- ¼ cup chopped fresh parsley
- 1 tablespoon lemon juice
- 1 teaspoon salt
- ½ teaspoon pepper

Preheat oven to 325 degrees F. Remove neck, giblets, and liver from the turkey. Rinse turkey in cold water, pat dry with paper towels, and place in a shallow roasting pan.

In a large mixing bowl, stir together butter and minced garlic.

Add parsley to the butter mixture.

Add lemon juice, salt, and pepper and mix until combined.

Carefully separate the skin from the turkey, being careful not to remove or tear the skin. Use your hands to spread ⅔ of the butter mixture under the skin and directly on the turkey breast.

Rub remaining butter over the outside skin of the entire turkey. Season with additional salt and pepper, if desired.

Create a tent of aluminum foil over the outside of the turkey, tucking the foil down the sides of the roasting pan. Be sure the shiny side of the foil is facing in toward the turkey and the dull side is facing out.

Cook in preheated oven 2 hours for a 10- to 12-pound turkey, and an additional 15 minutes for each additional pound. Remove the foil and increase the oven temperature to 425 degrees F. Cook for 1 more hour, or until the internal temperature of the turkey breast registers at least 165 degrees F. and the internal temperature of the thighs registers 175 to 180 degrees F. (To read the temperature most accurately, be sure to insert thermometer in the thickest part of both the breast and the thigh, avoiding the bones in each.)

Let turkey rest, tented with foil, about 20 minutes and then cut into slices and serve.

*Note:* If using a frozen turkey, be sure to move turkey to the refrigerator at least 3 days before preparing to allow adequate time for the turkey to thaw.

# Pumpkin Spice Cheesecake

Serves: 12 | Prep time: 10 minutes | Cook time: 1 hour | Total time: 1 hour, 10 minutes

1   (15.25-ounce) box spice cake mix, prepared according to package directions

3   (8-ounce) packages cream cheese, softened

3   eggs

1   (15-ounce) can pumpkin

1   (14-ounce) can sweetened condensed milk

4   teaspoons pumpkin pie spice

Preheat oven to 350 degrees F. Spray a 10-inch springform pan with nonstick cooking spray. Prepare cake mix according to package directions. Pour 2½ cups cake batter into springform pan. Bake 15 to 17 minutes.

In a large mixing bowl, beat together cream cheese until fluffy. Beat in eggs, pumpkin, sweetened condensed milk, and pumpkin pie spice.

Pour cream cheese mixture over hot cake crust. Fill to about 1 inch from the top of the pan. Reduce oven to 300 degrees F. Bake 45 to 50 minutes, or until the center of the cheesecake is set and the edges are golden brown.

Let cool completely and serve.

# Turtle Pumpkin Pie

Serves: 8 | Prep time: 10 minutes | Cook time: n/a | Total time: 10 minutes

- ⅓ cup caramel ice cream topping
- 1 ready-to-use graham cracker crust
- ½ cup chopped pecans
- 2 (3.4-ounce) packages instant vanilla pudding mix
- 1 cup cold milk
- 1 cup canned pumpkin
- 1 teaspoon ground cinnamon
- ½ teaspoon ground nutmeg
- 1 (8-ounce) tub whipped nondairy topping, thawed

Pour caramel topping onto bottom of pie crust; sprinkle with pecans.

In a large bowl, beat together pudding mixes, milk, canned pumpkin, cinnamon, and nutmeg. Fold in 1½ cups whipped topping, then spoon mixture into the crust.

Refrigerate 1 hour.

Top pie with remaining whipped topping, then drizzle with additional caramel topping and pecans (optional) before serving.

# TRADITIONS

## Pie Party

Thanksgiving can get so crazy, and the last thing we want to do is spend more time in the kitchen than with the family. Our family started a new tradition of having a pie party. It's so much fun to get together as sisters with our mom and bake pies. It's also nice to enjoy Thanksgiving morning rather than slaving away in the kitchen making pies. We usually get together 3 to 4 days in advance and bake our favorite pies. Everyone brings all the ingredients they need for their own pie, then we listen to Christmas music and all make our pies together. Here is one of our favorites that always seems to make an appearance at our annual pie party!

### Caramel Apple Pie

Serves: 12 | Prep time: 20 minutes | Cook time: 1 hour | Total time: 1 hour, 20 minutes

| | |
|---|---|
| 1 | (16.5-ounce) can refrigerated sugar cookie dough |
| ½ | cup plus 2 tablespoons all-purpose flour, divided |
| 2½ | pounds Granny Smith or Honeycrisp apples, peeled, cored, and sliced thin |
| ½ | cup granulated sugar |
| 1½ | teaspoons apple pie spice |
| 1¼ | cups caramel ice cream topping, divided |
| 1 | recipe Crumb Topping |

Heat oven to 350 degrees F. Lightly spray a 10-inch springform pan or deep-dish pie pan with nonstick cooking spray.

Mix the cookie dough and ½ cup flour in a bowl until combined well. Press dough into the bottom of the pan, going up the sides of the pan about ¾ inch.

In a mixing bowl, toss the apples with sugar, 2 tablespoons flour, and apple pie spice and then turn into the prepared crust and spread out evenly. Drizzle ¾ cup caramel topping over the apple mixture. Cover with aluminum foil and cook 45 minutes.

Remove pie from oven and take off the foil. Sprinkle Crumb Mixture over the warm pie and return pie to oven uncovered. Continue baking an additional 15 to 20 minutes, or until the topping is lightly browned.

Allow the pie to cool and then remove springform pan sides. When ready to serve, slice the pie and then drizzle with remaining caramel topping.

## Crumb Topping

- 1 cup all-purpose flour
- ½ cup brown sugar
- ½ cup granulated sugar
- 1 teaspoon vanilla
- 1½ teaspoons apple pie spice
- ½ cup butter

In a small bowl, whisk together flour, brown sugar, sugar, vanilla, and apple pie spice. Cut in the butter with a fork, pastry cutter, or your hands and mix until it forms a wet crumb mixture.

# DECEMBER

*Festive Recipes for a Merry Christmas*

# Chocolate Reindeer Cookies

Serves: 24 | Prep time: 20 minutes | Cook time: 7 minutes | Total time: 27 minutes

1 (15.25-ounce) box Devil's Food cake mix

2 eggs

¾ cup vegetable shortening

1 small container chocolate frosting

1 bag holiday colored M&M's

24 mini vanilla wafer cookies

48 mini pretzel twists

48 edible eyes

Preheat oven to 350 degrees F.

Mix together cake mix, eggs, and shortening until well combined. The dough will be pretty thick.

Roll dough into 1-inch balls, making sure they are all similar in size. Place dough balls on ungreased cookie sheet and bake 8 minutes.

Immediately transfer cookies to a cooking rack.

Frost each cookie with chocolate frosting. Use frosting to place a vanilla wafer on the cookie for the reindeer snout. Stick an M&M's nose on the wafer with a small dab of chocolate frosting. Place the pretzels on for the antlers. And then place the edible eyes just above the wafer cookie.

# Christmas Tree Brownies

Serves: 9 | Prep time: 15 minutes | Cook time: 35 minutes | Total time: 50 minutes

1 (15-ounce) box brownie mix, prepared according to package directions

1 tablespoon butter (at room temperature)

1 (8-ounce) package cream cheese

1 teaspoon vanilla

1 teaspoon milk

3 cups powdered sugar

4 drops green food coloring

Sprinkles for garnish

Cut prepared and cooled brownies into triangles.

Place the cut brownies on parchment paper or a cooling rack so they can be easily removed without sticking.

In a medium-sized bowl, beat the butter, cream cheese, vanilla, and milk together until smooth. Add the powdered sugar and continue to beat until smooth and creamy, about 3 minutes. Add 4 drops green food coloring and continue to mix until the color is fully mixed in.

Scoop the frosting into a plastic zipper-top bag, seal bag, and cut a small hole in the corner. Pipe the frosting over the triangle brownie in a zigzag pattern. Add sprinkles for ornaments.

Refrigerate until ready to serve.

# Gingerbread Cheesecake Cookie Cups

Serves: 30 | Prep time: 10 minutes | Cook time: 8 minutes | Total time: 18 minutes

½ cup butter, melted

½ cup brown sugar

1 egg

½ cup dark molasses

2 cups all-purpose flour

2 teaspoons baking soda

1½ teaspoons ground ginger

2 teaspoons ground cinnamon, divided

½ teaspoon ground cloves

⅓ teaspoon salt

3 ounces cream cheese

2 cups powdered sugar

1 teaspoon vanilla extract

Preheat oven to 350 degrees F. and lightly grease a mini muffin tin.

In a large bowl with an electric mixer, beat together the butter, brown sugar, egg, and molasses until fully incorporated, smooth, and creamy.

Add the flour, baking soda, ginger, 1 teaspoon of the cinnamon, cloves, and salt until fully combined. Roll dough into 1-inch balls and place in the mini muffin tins.

Create an indent in each cookie by placing your thumb in each one.

Bake for 8 minutes (they may seem undercooked, but you don't want them burned).

Let cookies cool completely before frosting.

For the frosting, mix the cream cheese, powdered sugar, vanilla, and remaining 1 teaspoon cinnamon until fully combined.

Place a dollop of frosting on each cookie and sprinkle with cinnamon or sprinkles.

# Egg Nog French Toast

Serves: 6 | Prep time: 10 minutes | Cook time: 5 minutes | Total time: 15 minutes

10 to 12 slices thick white bread, such as Texas toast or French bread

2 eggs

2 cups egg nog

½ teaspoon ground cinnamon

¼ teaspoon ground nutmeg

½ teaspoon granulated sugar

Spray a large skillet with nonstick cooking spray. Heat skillet to medium heat. In a shallow dish, whisk together eggs, egg nog, cinnamon, nutmeg, and sugar. Dip each side of the bread into the mixture and cook in skillet for about 3 minutes on each side, or until golden brown. Serve with maple syrup.

# Pecan Shortbread Bars

Serves: 12 | Prep time: 15 minutes | Cook time: 35 minutes | Total time: 50 minutes

| | |
|---|---|
| 2 cups butter, softened and divided | 1 teaspoon vanilla |
| 1¾ cups all-purpose flour | 2 tablespoons heavy cream |
| ½ cup powdered sugar | 3 eggs, beaten |
| ½ cup corn syrup | 2 cups chopped pecans |
| 1 cup brown sugar | |

Preheat oven to 350 degrees F. Lightly grease a 9x13-inch pan and set aside.

In a large bowl, beat together 1 cup of the butter, the flour, and the powdered sugar until a thick dough forms. Press into bottom of prepared pan and bake 10 to 12 minutes, or until crust is set.

While crust is baking, melt remaining 1 cup butter and let cool slightly. Mix together melted butter, corn syrup, brown sugar, vanilla, heavy cream, and beaten eggs until smooth. Stir in the pecans. Pour over crust as soon as crust is done baking. Return to the oven for 25 minutes, or until middle is set. Cut into bars and serve after cooled.

# Gingerbread Loaf

Yield: 1 large loaf | Prep time: 10 minutes | Cook time: 55 minutes | Total time: 65 minutes

| | |
|---|---|
| 1½ cups all-purpose flour | 1 teaspoon baking soda |
| 2 teaspoons ground cinnamon | ½ cup butter, softened |
| 1 teaspoon ground cloves | 1 cup granulated sugar |
| 2¼ teaspoons ground ginger | 1 cup unsweetened applesauce |
| 1 teaspoon salt | 1 recipe Frosting for Gingerbread Loaf |

Preheat oven to 350 degrees F. Line a 9x5-inch loaf pan with foil and spray foil with nonstick cooking spray.

In a medium bowl, whisk together flour, cinnamon, cloves, ginger, salt, and baking soda. In a large bowl, cream together butter, sugar, and applesauce.

Add the dry ingredients to the wet ingredients and mix until combined. Pour mixture into prepared loaf pan.

Bake 45 to 55 minutes until a toothpick inserted in the center comes out clean. Let cool.

Once cool, spread frosting over top. Allow frosting to set up for 1 hour (you can put it in the refrigerator to speed up the process).

## Frosting for Gingerbread Loaf

| | |
|---|---|
| 3 tablespoons butter | ½ teaspoon vanilla |
| 2 ounces cream cheese | 4 to 6 tablespoons milk |
| 3 cups powdered sugar | |

In a medium bowl cream together butter, cream cheese, powdered sugar, vanilla, and milk until smooth. Allow to set up for 1 hour (you can put it in the refrigerator to speed up the process). Store any leftover frosting in an airtight container.

# Salted Nut Roll Fudge

Yields: 48 pieces | Prep time: 30 minutes | Cook time: 10 minutes | Total time: 40 minutes

## Fudge

- 2½ cups granulated sugar
- ½ cup butter
- ⅔ cup evaporated milk
- 8 ounces vanilla almond bark
- 1 (7-ounce) jar marshmallow crème
- 1 teaspoon vanilla extract

## Caramel Center

- ¼ cup butter
- ½ cup granulated sugar
- ½ cup light brown sugar
- ½ cup light corn syrup
- ½ cup sweetened condensed milk
- 1½ cups peanuts

For fudge: Line a 9x13-inch pan with aluminum foil and spray foil with nonstick cooking spray. In a large saucepan, combine sugar, butter, and ⅔ cup evaporated milk. Cook over medium heat until sugar is dissolved, being sure to stir occasionally to prevent burning. Bring to a boil and stir occasionally for 7 minutes. Remove from heat and stir in almond bark and marshmallow crème until smooth. Stir in vanilla extract until well combined. Pour half the fudge mixture into the bottom of prepared pan.

To prepare caramel center: In a large, microwave-safe bowl, melt butter, sugars, corn syrup, and sweetened condensed milk on high power for 2 minutes. Stir well and heat another 2 minutes. Stir again, return to microwave, and heat a final 2 minutes. Stir until smooth and then pour over the fudge mixture in pan. Spread peanuts over the caramel and lightly press them into the caramel mixture. Pour the second half of the fudge mixture over top and sprinkle with any remaining peanuts. Chill in the refrigerator for 2 hours, or until fudge is set. Cut into squares and serve.

## TRADITIONS

*12 Days of Hot Cocoa*

There's nothing better than warming up with a cup of hot cocoa on a cold day! We've created 12 simple hot chocolate recipes that you can make by adding just a few ingredients to a mug of prepared hot chocolate! Follow our recipe for Basic Homemade Hot Chocolate and then simply add in the ingredients called for in the 12 variations that follow.

## Basic Homemade Hot Chocolate

| | | | |
|---|---|---|---|
| ½ | cup granulated sugar | ⅓ | cup hot water |
| ¼ | cup unsweetened cocoa powder | 1 | teaspoon vanilla extract |
| ⅛ | teaspoon salt | 4 | cups milk |

Combine sugar, cocoa, and salt in a medium saucepan. Whisk in water and cook over medium heat, stirring constantly, until mixture comes to a boil. Boil and stir constantly for 2 minutes. Whisk in milk and warm to desired serving temperature. Remove from heat and whisk in vanilla.

### 1. Raspberry Hot Chocolate

1 cup Basic Homemade Hot Chocolate

⅛ teaspoon raspberry extract

4 to 5 fresh raspberries, for garnish

1 chocolate raspberry stick, for stirring

### 2. Red Velvet Hot Chocolate

1 cup Basic Homemade Hot Chocolate

2 tablespoons red velvet cake mix

White chocolate chips, for garnish

### 3. Egg Nog Hot Chocolate

½ cup Basic Homemade Hot Chocolate

½ cup egg nog, warmed

Whipped cream, for topping

Dash nutmeg, for garnish

### 4. Caramel Hot Chocolate

1 cup Basic Homemade Hot Chocolate

3 ROLO candies

1 to 2 teaspoons caramel syrup, for garnish

### 5. S'mores Hot Chocolate

1 cup Basic Homemade Hot Chocolate

4 large marshmallows, toasted with a lighter or blowtorch

Graham cracker crumbs, for garnish

### 6. Dark Chocolate Hot Chocolate

1 cup Basic Homemade Hot Chocolate

1 square Ghirardelli dark chocolate

Mini dark chocolate chips, for garnish

### 7. Candy Cane Hot Chocolate

1 cup Basic Homemade Hot Chocolate

⅛ teaspoon peppermint extract

Whipped cream, for topping

Crushed candy canes, for garnish

1 candy cane, for stirring

### 8. Pumpkin Spice Hot Chocolate

1 cup Basic Homemade Hot Chocolate

½ tablespoon pumpkin puree

Whipped cream, for topping

Dash of pumpkin pie spice, for garnish

### 9. White Chocolate Hot Chocolate

1 cup Basic Homemade Hot Chocolate

Mini-marshmallows

2 Hershey's Cookies n' Cream fun-sized candy bars, coarsely chopped

1 to 2 teaspoons melted white chocolate, for garnish

### 10. Cookies and Cream Hot Chocolate

1 cup Basic Homemade Hot Chocolate

Mini-marshmallows

4 crushed Oreos

1 to 2 teaspoons chocolate syrup, for garnish

### 11. Nutella Hot Chocolate

1 cup Basic Homemade Hot Chocolate

1 tablespoon Nutella

Chocolate Hazelnut Pirouette cookie, for garnish and stirring

### 12. Chocolate Orange

1 cup Basic Homemade Hot Chocolate

$\frac{1}{8}$ teaspoon orange extract

1 chocolate orange stick, for stirring

# INDEX

References to page numbers with photographs are in **bold**.

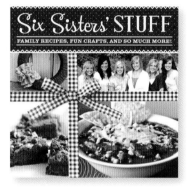

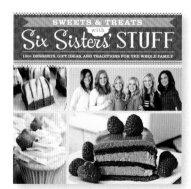
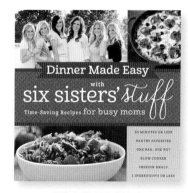